THE AMAZON
AND THE PAGE

THE AMAZON
AND THE PAGE

Natalie Clifford Barney
and Renée Vivien

KARLA JAY

INDIANA UNIVERSITY PRESS
Bloomington and Indianapolis

Manufactured in the United States of America

Library of Congress Cataloging-in-Publication Data

Jay, Karla.
The amazon and the page.

Bibliography: p.
Includes index.
1. Barney, Natalie Clifford.   2. Vivien, Renée,
1877–1909.   3. French literature—Women authors—
History and criticism.   4. Women and literature—
France—History.   5. Feminism and literature—France—
History.   6. Women authors, French—Biography.
7. Lesbians—France—Biography.   8. France—Exiles—
Biography.   I. Title.
PQ3939.B3Z72   1988   840'.9'9287   87-45405
ISBN 0-253-30408-3
0-253-20476-3 (pbk.)
1   2   3   4   5   92 91 90 89 88

For my father, and in memory of my mother

CONTENTS

ACKNOWLEDGMENTS

There are many people to thank for a work that has taken over a decade to complete, and it is impossible to mention everyone who has provided emotional and scholarly support over the years. I would, however, especially like to thank the following: François Chapon and Nicole Prévot of the Bibliothèque Doucet for allowing me access to the Barney legacy; the Bibliothèque Nationale for access to the letters of Renée Vivien; William E. Huntington for permission to cite from the published work of Natalie Barney and the unpublished work of Alice Pike Barney; Jean Chalon, Berthe Cleyrergue, Renée O'Brien, and Simone Burgues for allowing me to interview them and/or to view their private collections; the late Dr. Jeannette H. Foster for her pioneering research on Barney and Vivien and for her gift to me of the original editions of their work without which this book would have been difficult to research; Joanne Glasgow, Barbara Lekatsas, and Sharon Spencer, for providing invaluable scholarly support; Monte Hewson and Blanche Amelkin for word processing assistance; and the Scholarly Research Committee and Summer Research Grant Program of Pace University and the Gay Academic Union for financial support. I would also like to extend my gratitude to the many people who gave me havens in which to work over the years, including Marie-José and Louis Barcet and Patricia Bailey. Finally, my deepest appreciation goes to Yvonne M. Klein for her endless good advice and to Mgt. Desmond, who gave me the courage and faith to complete this work.

INTRODUCTION

Now that the early years of the second wave of the feminist movement have elapsed, it no longer seems enough merely to rediscover lost women writers who had disappeared among the dusty shelves of secondhand bookstores and the storage stacks of libraries. Now that more of these writers emerge from their ill-deserved obscurity, it becomes increasingly possible to attempt to establish connections among them as well as to investigate the sources of their ideas, their stylistic preoccupations, and the literary and intellectual contributions they have made.

In this context, the works of Natalie Clifford Barney and Renée Vivien (Pauline Mary Tarn) are a particularly fruitful area of feminist scholarship, especially in view of the fact that, in general, commentators on both of these writers have been more interested in documenting the peculiarities of their respective styles of life rather than in paying serious attention to their literary sources, concerns, and innovations. The very titles of the longer and more popular books on the two women give an indication of the major preoccupations of their authors. Some of the titles include: Yves-Gérard Le Dantec's *Renée Vivien: femme damnée, femme sauvée (Renée Vivien: Woman Damned, Woman Saved)* and Jean Chalon's biography of Barney, *Portrait d'une séductrice (Portrait of a Seductress)*. There is little in these titles or between the covers of any of these books to suggest that Barney and Vivien present anything but a purely anecdotal interest.

Both Natalie Barney and Renée Vivien deserve to be seen as more than the rather spicy literary footnotes they seem to have become. Both were prolific writers. Barney produced twenty volumes, most of them in French, which exhibit a remarkable diversity of genre and subject: poems, plays, epigrams, essays, portraits of her contemporaries, and a novel. Renée Vivien, who died at the age of thirty-two, published more than nine volumes of poetry, one novel (a second was in preparation at the time of her death), and two volumes of prose—all in French. In addition, she translated Sappho from Greek into French.

Both women enjoyed a brief burst of recognition, then sank into obscurity. In part, the lack of first-hand knowledge of their work is attributable to the fact that a great deal of it was, until recently, out of print and still remains so. Researching their work and lives, therefore, became a difficult, but rewarding, task.

My own research into their lives and work has taken over ten years. I first heard about them in a paper delivered by Gayle Rubin at a Gay Academic Union Conference in New York City in 1973. In 1975 Jonathan Katz asked me to read all of the works of Barney and Vivien and to choose two by each author for a series of books on homosexuality that Arno Press was about to issue. As I read their works, I began to see an intriguing interrelationship between the two authors that consisted of common themes, patterns, archetypes, and even the titles of works. About the same time, the late Jeannette H. Foster, who had written the pioneering work, *Sex-Variant Women in Literature,* gave me her French library, which included some first editions by Barney and Vivien.

It seemed that Jeannette Foster had bequeathed a rare legacy to me that I wanted to carry forward. I stopped research on a Comparative Literature dissertation on the Theater of the Absurd (besides, Beckett and Ionesco were writing faster than I was!) and switched my thesis to these two expatriate women. At that time, when almost no one had heard of Natalie Barney and few had read Renée Vivien, it was not easy to persuade either my department or typical patriarchal granting sources that these women were worthy of serious consideration. Nevertheless, their concepts continued to intrigue me, and I persisted in my research, including several trips to France. Investigating their lives did not prove to be easy. Renée Vivien's papers passed into the possession of Salomon Reinach, who later deposited them in the Bibliothèque Nationale, where they have been sealed, along with his own papers, until the year 2000 (and I did hope to be finished before then). Reinach, who was a friend of Vivien, appears to have been motivated by the desire to protect her literary reputation as well as the personal reputations of those who had known her intimately. It is, of course, useless to speculate at this point about the nature of the material which persuaded Reinach to seal her papers until ninety years after Vivien's death. Natalie Barney was among those who disagreed with Reinach's decision: "In my opinion, he is protecting a reputation that he should spread rather than defend."[1] She was curious about how the removal of Vivien's papers from the eyes of scholars could possibly "protect" or "enhance" the reputation of a poet already experiencing waning public recognition. She suggested that Reinach's silencing of Vivien's unpublished voice constituted a graver indiscretion than any openness might: "In terms of the past which is truly past, discretion is only valueless obliteration. There is also the indiscretion of silence. And wouldn't it be a hopeless cowardice to let our dead die?"[2] Fortunately, some other material survived. Most helpful were a bundle of letters she had written to a French poet, Amédée Moullé, which I located in the Bibliothèque Nationale.

Natalie Barney willed her letters, papers, and unpublished manuscripts to the Bibliothèque Doucet in Paris so that they would be available to scholars and would not meet the same fate as Vivien's documents. Since Barney reached an advanced age, she had amassed an enormous correspondence consisting of over forty thousand letters; these took several years to catalog. She had once warned her biographer Jean Chalon, "My disorder is inexhaustible; don't let it exhaust you."[3] Regardless, François Chapon and Nicole Prévot of the Bibliothèque Doucet undertook the gargantuan task. Jean Chalon also had been given a number of letters by Barney before her death, though she had destroyed many others.[4]

Fortunately, by 1978, the Barney legacy had finally been catalogued. François Chapon, Barney's literary executor, graciously permitted me to read the unpublished manuscripts as well as letters to and from her mother, Alice Pike Barney, and to and from her sister, Laura Dreyfus-Barney. Regrettably, because French law allows the reading of letters of deceased persons only upon the permission of the estate of the writer, it was not possible to examine letters written by others, such as Colette and the Duchess de Clermont-Tonnerre.

It was, however, possible to interview several of Barney's friends, including Jean Chalon, and Barney's housekeeper for over half a century, Berthe Cleyrergue. I was also able to examine their personal libraries which contained copies of Barney's works and those of other authors annotated in her own hand, as well as to read extremely rare copies of privately printed works, such as "The Woman Who Lives with Me." Other friends and acquaintances of Barney were similarly generous in allowing me to examine original editions and holographs by both Barney and Vivien. Renée O'Brien, the niece of Renée Vivien, was particularly helpful in recounting her family history. These primary sources form the basis of the present study.

An examination of this mass of material, especially those documents heretofore unseen by other scholars, led to the conviction that a serious reevaluation of the work of Barney and Vivien and of their literary relationship to one another was necessary. It also became apparent that Barney and Vivien were a rich topic of study for a feminist: They presented an interesting example of fruitful literary connection, one in which, evidently, Natalie Barney was a chief source of theoretical inspira-

tion to Renée Vivien, who worked out the implications of Barney's Les-
bian/feminism in her fiction, although Vivien in turn broadened the
thematic scope of Barney's work. Furthermore, in their concern for the
invention of new models and myths for women, Barney and Vivien
anticipated some of the concerns of contemporary French and American
feminist writers.

But above all, it is in their partial failure as well as in their success that
these two writers are significant to the contemporary reader. They were
each committed to the full-scale redemption of the entire weight of
Western literature and myth to serve their woman-centered philosophy.
They ransacked the pages of history to find appropriate heroines for a
women's literature. They sought to convert the conventions of courtly
love to serve a new religion of love. They transformed the images of the
Symbolist poetry they adored into an expression of a spiritual transcendence achieved through the devotion to an unapproachable woman. They
daringly created a new approach to gender, sex, and sexual preference in a
time when most of their contemporaries discussed the subject apolo-
getically. Moreover, they pragmatically sought ways in which their theoretical ideas could be actualized. Of all the American and British
expatriates of their era, they alone expressed their allegiance to an international community of letters and their liberation from patriarchal concerns of nationalism by writing in French. Inevitably, so audacious a
literary and philosophical undertaking could not altogether succeed, but
the degree of their intellectual attainment is remarkable.

It is precisely because of the magnitude of their challenge to conventional assumptions about the position and creative potentiality of
women that Vivien and Barney were not able fully to achieve their
ambitions. They were both women of immensely privileged backgrounds,
a situation which led them to underestimate the importance of social and
economic necessity in the actual lives of the mass of women. They were
also remarkably isolated from both historical and contemporary relations
with other women writers and/or feminists. Though both mention dozens of male writers whom they had read and who influenced them, prior
to 1909 neither appears to have read much of any woman writer with the
exception of Sappho. They obviously felt that they, like she, would be
privileged enough to be accepted by the male literary establishment
whereas the emulation of nineteenth-century women writers, such as the
Brontës, would negatively categorize them as "women writers." Moreover, they were completely out of touch with the Bloomsbury group in
England, a fact which has startled many who know of their work, for the

similarities both of theme and lifestyle (their literary groups, for example) are striking. As a result, they stand outside the female literary tradition as delineated by Sandra Gilbert and Susan Gubar, among others, and often must be viewed in relation to male French Symbolist predecessors rather than to the canon of women writers, for the similarities to the latter are, alas, accidental.

They also believed that symbol and myth were fully detachable from the social context which had given rise to them. As a result, their attempt to reclaim these images for a new and positive women-centered literature was not altogether successful, since they tended unwittingly to adopt the assumptions which underlay these images and to apply them uncritically to the new forms of relations which they were seeking to invent.

Nevertheless, both Natalie Barney and Renée Vivien developed ideas and adopted literary stances which had never before been explored in quite the same way. Although these two authors frequently borrowed from Sappho and the Symbolists, they always transformed their material into a style and a substance which were unmistakably their own, and which opened up a new terrain for other feminist writers with similar concerns.

Although no claim may be made that either Natalie Barney or Renée Vivien was a writer of the first rank, both women were unquestionably serious artists whose works are long overdue for reconsideration. Their almost uncanny anticipation of the preoccupations of feminist writers whose work began almost sixty years after Vivien's death gives them a place as foremothers of feminist literature, though foremothers who have been sadly overlooked.

There is considerable irony in the fact that these women who so diligently sought to rediscover lost women of the distant past, like Vashti and Lilith, should, in so short a space of time, have almost become lost themselves. Barney and Vivien touched upon many topics of interest to linguists, historians, and cultural anthropologists, as well as literary historians. They have opened up provocative areas of investigation for anyone who, like themselves, is willing to imagine the world from a gynocentric point of view, and by doing so, they have established a strong and permanent place for themselves as harbingers of a new age in women's literature.

I.

THE AMAZON AND THE PAGE

Many authors are so well-known to us that it is quite unnecessary to begin a literary study with biography. With Natalie Clifford Barney and Renée Vivien, however, the case is quite different. For one thing, no biography of Renée Vivien exists in English. For another, the two biographies of Natalie Barney—*The Amazon of Letters* by George Wickes and *Portrait of a Seductress* by Jean Chalon—are both commercially oriented works by male authors who show themselves to be far more interested in the titillating aspects of the lives of these two women than in their literary environs or in a feminist analysis of their lives. In addition, it is unquestionably true that even among feminists, far more have heard about these two women than have actually read anything about them. What is often recounted to me are bits of biography so blown out of proportion that Barney becomes Amazonian beyond her wildest dreams, while Vivien becomes a figure straight from the works of Poe, haunted mercilessly by the spectre of looming death. It is necessary, therefore, to correct the mythology which has not only gone too often unchallenged in the feminist community but which, as we shall see, has been exaggerated or misinterpreted in some cases by well-meaning critics.

There is also the inescapable fact that Barney and Vivien felt that their work had to be *lived* in order to be valid; in other words, they "field tested" their ideas, so to speak. Although their inspirations worked much better in the imagination than on paper or in real life, there was an unbreakable connection for them between life and art.

Many students are still taught that the interpretation of a work must rely on pure deconstruction or on the semiotics of the work. Many feminist critics, on the other hand, such as Sandra Gilbert, Susan Gubar, Jane Marcus, and Shari Benstock, have seen that for women writers the link between life and art is often inescapable. Women's writing is often more autobiographical, not only in form (for example, diaries and letters) but also in content. For Barney and Vivien the two are barely separable,

1

for their work evolved directly from their lives as their lives evolved directly from their artistic conception of themselves. To separate the two is as unthinkable as separating twins joined by one heart.

Natalie Clifford Barney was born in Dayton, Ohio on 31 October 1876—Halloween. Her father, the enormously wealthy Albert Clifford Barney, inherited a railroad car company from his father and then quickly sold it to the Pullman Sleeping Car Corporation. Alice Pike Barney, the heir to a whiskey fortune, was an accomplished portrait painter. Both families had a tradition of philanthropy and an interest in the arts. The family trust eventually left Natalie and her sister, Laura, with a fortune of well over three and a half million dollars apiece.[1]

Natalie Barney's early childhood was spent in Cincinnati where she learned French from her governess and from two childhood friends, Mary and Violet Shilleto. She may have taken a trip to Paris as early as 1883. Her family moved to Washington, D.C. around 1886, and they spent their summers on their Bar Harbor, Maine property, which they called Ban-y-Bryn. In either 1886 or 1887, the Barneys made a second trip to Europe. On different occasions young Natalie toured through Western Europe, Scandinavia, and Russia; in the last country the great poverty of the people seemed to have made a lasting impression on her. "I was so overwhelmed by the underground dwellings of the poor—worse than tanneries for animals—that when we returned in the evening, I told our governess that I would not leave this unfortunate country before having helped the people."[2] She also became particularly aware of the plight of women; for example, in Belgium she was appalled by a dog and woman pulling a cart while the man strode alongside. "It was at that moment," she declared, "that we [Laura and Natalie] became feminists."[3]

Albert Barney returned to the United States while Alice settled in Paris and studied painting with Carolus-Duran.[4] Natalie and Laura were sent off to a select boarding school, Les Ruches, which was later made notorious by Dorothy Strachey's scandalous autobiography, Olivia, which vividly described her Lesbian relationships there.[5] Barney regretted that she had not been in Strachey's class.

Accompanied by her mother and sister, Natalie traveled several times between Paris and Bar Harbor or Washington. In 1898 they all returned to Paris so that Alice could study painting with Whistler. Alice was apparently quite independent by nature and lived as she chose. Though Albert occasionally tried to assert his patriarchal authority over the family, Alice tended to act independently of his wishes, and Natalie emulated her mother's philosophical stance that it was important to live as one wished. Albert, though occasionally irate and eager to reassert his will, generally let Alice go her own way, so long as she did not create a public scandal. From her mother, Natalie learned to placate her father, though she did so as rarely as possible.

By 1899, Natalie had already had several Lesbian affairs, including one with Evalina Palmer, heiress to a biscuit fortune. The Belgian ambassador, because of Natalie's attachment to Eva and piqued by Natalie's evident disinterest in him, used a homophobic term to describe Natalie. The word, which Natalie does not repeat, made her realize that she was a Lesbian. She was shocked by having to acknowledge her own "deviance"; as a result, she briefly withdrew from Eva and from men, but later Eva would play an important role in Natalie's life.[6] Also during this period, Natalie became engaged to Freddy Manners-Sutton.

Natalie's first important affair was with Liane de Pougy, the most famous courtesan of the 1890s. In her autobiographical works, Natalie claims that she was motivated by a desire to help Liane and others "become what they really were."[7] In her opinion, Liane was not her true self and needed to be rescued "from a life that . . . [Natalie] judged to be unworthy of her."[8] Natalie was willing to "sacrifice" herself to the extent of marrying Manners-Sutton to secure her dowry and a large living allowance in order to support Liane. Her fiancé apparently agreed to the unusual terms of Natalie's plan for a "Boston marriage." Liane, however, was quite enjoying her lifestyle, as well as her notoriety, and was not interested in Natalie's strategy for her "salvation." Later on, Liane married Prince George Ghika and abandoned her career in the demimonde.

Later, Natalie brought home a second suitor, Lord Alfred Douglas (whom Albert Barney naturally rejected instantly as a worthy suitor for his daughter).[9] Barney was motivated more by an ardent desire to free herself financially from the power of her father than by a desire to accommodate herself to his patriarchal demands, as Shari Benstock suggests.[10] In her latter engagement, there is even a suggestion of mocking the entire notion of marriage by coming up with such an obviously undesirable suitor. Her engagement to Bosie made Albert Barney realize that he did not want his daughter married to just any man and that perhaps spinsterhood was preferable to Natalie's taste in men!

Despite Natalie's familial difficulties and the sometimes stormy nature of her affair with Liane de Pougy, two positive literary works emerged from this Lesbian relationship: Pougy's *L'Idylle saphique (Sapphic Idyll)* and Barney's first book of poems. Liane de Pougy's novel, published in

1901, contained the story of the liaison, and Natalie Barney collaborated on several chapters. Barney's first book written entirely by herself, *Quelques portraits-sonnets de femmes (Some Portraits and Sonnets of Women)* was published a year earlier. It contained a number of poems praising the beauty of women. Both books caused quite a stir because of their apparent lesboerotic content. Barney's poems received vicious reviews in the United States, especially one in *Town Topics* entitled "Sapho [sic] Sings in Washington": The reference to Sappho was not intended to flatter. Albert Barney bought up whatever copies he could find of the book and destroyed the plates.[11] This time young Natalie had gone too far, and her father exercised his patriarchal authority in a way that a man of his wealth and social position could—he obliterated her work by making it both unavailable and too expensive and dangerous to reprint.

It is interesting to note that Alice Barney illustrated the book with portraits of women, some of them Natalie's lovers. She seems to have condoned Natalie's Lesbianism so long as Natalie was discreet about it— that is, kept her affairs in the closet. But when Natalie's sexual liaisons left the private domain, she was just as appalled as Albert. In this regard, Shari Benstock's creation of a rather typical feminist dichotomy between the bad patriarch and the supportive matriarch is simply not upheld by the correspondence between Natalie and her mother.[12] In a letter dated 25 January 1901, Alice referred to previous scandals Natalie had caused in Bar Harbor and complained that now Albert Barney and "his mother and sister are *alone*—more shunned than if they had killed some one [sic] (for that is an impulse perhaps—and it has not the horror that this has). . . . But you must make yourself a horror. . . ."[13] That Alice considered murder less abhorrent than Lesbianism is a revealing comment on the mores of the Victorian era, in which murder was less premeditated than a sexual act. Natalie, despite her great affection for her mother, was characteristically unapologetic about her behavior: Though she did make half-hearted attempts to marry, she never apologized for her Lesbian inclinations, labeling herself "naturally unnatural."[14]

When the brouhaha died down, Natalie and Alice returned to an affectionate relationship, and Albert again left them alone. Natalie called her mother by endearments such as "Muz-buz," "Dear Little One," and "Mother-Bird."[15] They collaborated on an unpublished play, "The Color of His Soul," and its Wildean wit was emulated by Natalie in her later plays and epigrams. Alice also continued to paint Natalie's lovers. It was in part Alice's nurturance of her daughter's artistic proclivities that not only encouraged her to develop as a writer but also inspired her later to nurture other women in turn in her salon and her Academy of Women.

One of Alice's portraits was of Renée Vivien, whom Natalie also met in 1899, through their mutual friends, Violet and Mary Shilleto. Renée Vivien admired the four poems in the manuscript of *Some Portraits and Sonnets* that deal with sadness and death. Barney was struck by Vivien's sadness and longing for death and transferred her need to save Liane to a protective love for Renée.

Renée Vivien's early years are not nearly so well documented. She was born Pauline Mary Tarn in Paddington, England on 11 June 1877, although most accounts incorrectly place her birth in the United States. Her father, John Tarn, "came of North Country farming stock, which had also been connected with the then properous [sic] lead mining area in Teesdale and Swalesdale."[16] Her mother, Mary Gillet Bennett, was an American, whose family was from Jackson, Michigan, near Detroit. Vivien's parents met in Hawaii, and after they were married on 16 August 1876 in Honolulu, they returned to London. Mrs. Tarn "became a British subject on marriage and travelled on a British passport."[17] In letters written in 1894, Vivien recounted that the family fortune was created by her paternal grandfather who had turned a small store into a chain of department stores. Vivien's father's primary interest seemed to be in horseracing. About a year after Vivien's birth, the family moved to Paris, where Vivien's sister, Antoinette, was born in 1881. The two young girls had an English governess and "attended French classes held in a street off the Rond-Point of the Champs-Elysées."[18]

Vivien had unhappy recollections of her childhood: "I began to live at the age of fourteen. Until then, I had only a very sad childhood. As a small child, I was subject to the tyranny of horrid German maids who terrorized me—I was constantly punished or scolded. I was always afraid."[19]

Part of Vivien's education was in Paris, where she once lived next door to Mary and Violet Shilleto. Vivien developed an unconsummated passion for Violet which lasted the rest of her life and which played a major role in her poetry, much of which is about Violet and violets. Vivien also traveled to Norway, Switzerland, Italy, and other countries.

Like many girls of the Victorian era, Vivien seems to have had little, if any, formal education. She read haphazardly whatever she chanced upon in the libraries of family members or of friends. She read almost exclusively in French, devouring Victor Hugo, Emile Zola, and Anatole France, though she did read some English Romantic poets, especially

Byron and Keats. Vivien was also an accomplished pianist, preferring Chopin and Beethoven above all other composers.

As a lonely and alienated six-year-old child, Vivien began writing stories to entertain herself, and at the age of nine she created some love poems for a childhood friend, Blanche. When she was fourteen, her first serious verse was inspired by a trip to Fontainbleau. She was about to destroy the poem when a female friend (probably Violet) persuaded her to keep it and to continue writing.

Vivien's father died when she was nine. Some time afterward, she returned to London with her mother and her sister, Antoinette. She fell into despair when she learned that she had to leave France, which she considered her native country. She knew no one in England other than a few relations, with whom she was soon on bad terms.

Vivien's relationship with her mother was never warm, and Vivien felt that her mother preferred Antoinette, who, according to Vivien, was not only the younger but the more attractive of the two sisters. After their return to England, however, tensions between mother and daughter increased. According to Vivien's niece, Renée O'Brien, Mrs. Tarn resented Vivien because she was rebellious and made her mother look old. In her mother's presence, Vivien suffered from headaches, vertigo, and sporadic fevers. She realized that her illnesses were psychosomatic and felt that "continual vexations, continual suffering, sorrow, and revolt can undermine even the most solid state of health." She added, "If only I could live as I like,"[20] by which she meant returning to France.

Vivien consoled herself by developing an intense correspondence with a fifty-year-old French poet, Amédée Moullé. He critiqued her poetry and presented her with books by Chateaubriand and other Romantic writers. Perhaps sensing that Vivien would do anything to escape from England and the clutches of her mother, Moullé proposed to her, but Vivien flatly and angrily rejected him:

> What devil had made you speak to me of *marriage?* . . . My mother, who has had sad enough experience with it, has told me that she would rather see me buried than married. . . . She is the only person around me who has good sense. Love and marriage, all that is good for people who have nothing else to do or who deserve some extremely harsh punishment.[21]

Despite this angry rejection and the formal *vous* Vivien used in her letters to him, Moullé had reason to hope, for Vivien referred to him as her "fiancé" in her poems and sent him what can only be described as love letters. Her mother had good cause to oppose any marriage plans that young Vivien might harbor, for the latter's paternal grandfather had left his estate to Pauline and Antoinette Tarn, and the money would pass to them upon their marriage or when they reached their majority.[22]

For a while, Vivien lived happily in the countryside in Shepperton with Antoinette, with whom she got on well. There, Vivien contentedly wrote poetry and read French writers, while her mother was supposedly traveling in Norway. But it turned out that her mother had never undertaken the trip, and the situation rapidly deteriorated once the family was reunited in London. Suspicious that Vivien was planning to flee to Paris and/or elope with Moullé, Mary Tarn locked Vivien up "as in a jail. All the doors of the house was [sic] locked."[23] Finally, Vivien escaped through an open window. After pawning a brooch, she had enough money to pay for lodging for five days and eat one meal a day. Just as she had run out of money and was about to throw herself into the Thames, she was discovered by one of her mother's maids. This is the story as Vivien recounts it, and it seems a bit theatrical. Probably, it was more likely that Vivien ran out of money and returned to her mother's home, however reluctantly.

According to Vivien, her mother tried to drive her insane in order to have her committed to a mental institution, after which she would procure Vivien's inheritance for herself, since Mrs. Tarn had no money of her own. To this end, she encouraged all Vivien's eccentricities and constantly told Vivien stories of insane relatives, including her father, who had apparently died in a state of delirium tremens (cause unspecified, though in his recent biography of Renée Vivien, Jean-Paul Goujon asserts that the true cause of death was the aftermath of a chill, which John Tarn caught by bathing in the sea near Etretat in September 1886).[24] The day of Vivien's disappearance, Mrs. Tarn rushed out to tell all their relatives that her elder daughter had escaped in a fit of madness.

Vivien's doctors were not convinced that the young poet was mad, so the case was eventually turned over to the courts. Although Mrs. Tarn had evidence that Pauline had once tried to commit suicide in Paris by taking chloroform, Vivien won the case and became a ward of the court. She was given a good legal guardian, of whom she was quite fond. He bought her fine dresses and gave her all the pocket money she wanted. She was happy at last, except that she was unable to leave England despite her new legal status.

She finally achieved some reconciliation with her mother, perhaps after her mother remarried an older, wealthy man. She remained on friendly terms with Antoinette and was the maid of honor at her wedding. Once

she had reached her majority, however, she permanently left the country
and the relatives she so vehemently detested.

Like Natalie Barney, Renée Vivien made her way to Paris at the turn of
the century. That American and British writers made a mecca of Paris at
the end of the nineteenth century and the beginning of the twentieth is a
fact that needs no elaboration. Oscar Wilde, Lord Alfred Douglas, James
Joyce, Ernest Hemingway, Sinclair Lewis, F. Scott Fitzgerald, Ezra Pound,
Radclyffe Hall, Lady Una Troubridge, Djuna Barnes, Janet Flanner,
Gertrude Stein, Alice B. Toklas, Edith Wharton . . . the long and impressive list goes on.

Their reasons for going to Paris were diverse. Some consciously adopted
the role of exile, like Joyce. For him, as for others, such as Gertrude Stein,
Paris was a city from which they could better view their own country and
its habits. There were also economic considerations: For the less rich,
like Gertrude Stein, the often-devalued French franc made living in Paris
a good bargain. For others, Paris was at once an adventure and an escape
from middle-class American Philistinism. Many writers went to Paris for
its relaxed moral atmosphere as compared to the Puritanism of the
United States and the Protestant rigidity of Great Britain. As Gertrude
Stein so aptly noted, it wasn't what Paris gave you, it was what Paris
didn't take away.[25]

It was primarily this moral freedom that attracted women such as
Renée Vivien and Natalie Clifford Barney, for with their hefty inheri-
tances, they could live wherever they chose. In her published memoirs,
Barney celebrated the fact that in Paris she was a free individual.

> Paris has always seemed to me the only city in which one can express
> oneself as one pleases. In spite of harmful progress inflicted from abroad, it
> continues to respect and even to encourage personality. In France thought,
> food, and love have remained a matter of personal taste and one's own
> business. . . .[26]

There are, as can be seen from these remarks, several aspects to Barney's
interpretation of moral freedom. Foremost is the right to live as one
wants. For Natalie Barney, Renée Vivien, Gertrude Stein, and Alice B.
Toklas, that included the right to be homosexual,[27] which was condoned
in France at that time.

Of course, Barney, Vivien, and Stein were not the first or the only ones
to seek out Paris for its laissez-faire attitude toward homosexuals. Earlier,
Oscar Wilde and Lord Alfred Douglas were virtually forced into exile

there because of the sexual scandal surrounding their lives in London and Wilde's imprisonment in Reading Gaol. As late as 1929, after the publication of and trials surrounding *The Well of Loneliness* in England and in the United States, Radclyffe Hall and her lover, Lady Una Troubridge, fled to the sanctuary of Paris, which they had visited in 1921. As Natalie Barney summed it up in a poem entitled "Love's Comrades" in *Poems & poèmes: autres alliances (Poems & Poèmes: Other Alliances):* "You say, I've lived too long in France . . . ? / I fear no country's ready yet / For our complexities. . . ."[28]

While Paris was not exactly a homosexual paradise nor precisely as depicted in Marcel Proust's *Remembrance of Things Past*, where every major character (except the narrator, Swann, and Françoise) turns out to be homosexual,[29] Barney and Vivien did find Paris to be full of lovely women who shared their predilection, and it was there that they found one another, too. When Violet and Mary Shilleto introduced Vivien to Barney, it was a case of "love at first sight." Vivien, who was to mythologize their romance in *Une Femme m'apparut . . . (A Woman Appeared to Me)*, a Symbolist *roman à clef* published in 1904, has her narrator faithfully recount that moment. "I evoke that distant hour when I saw her for the first time, and the shiver which ran down my spine when my eyes met her eyes of mortal steel, her eyes which were as sharp and blue as a blade. . . . The charm of peril emanated from her and drew me inexorably."[30] Since Vivien's novel was probably written after their relationship had permanently terminated, this description, as well as others in the novel, intermingles her initial joy with later bitterness.

As were so many others before and after her, Vivien was attracted to Barney's beauty—the pale blue eyes and thick, wavy blond hair. Liane de Pougy had already nicknamed her "Moonbeam" because of her iridescent, golden hair, and both of them also called Barney "Loreley," for the siren-like effect she had on other women and men, as well. A horseback riding enthusiast, Barney was agile and graceful.

In their attempts to insist that Barney was a Dona Juana, extant biographies of her tend to overemphasize her physical qualities while failing to note that she attracted both women and men well into her eighties when her appearance was somewhat dowdy and long after her famed blond hair had paled to a distant memory. Such accounts also tend to underplay Barney's charisma, which made her appear even more charming and beautiful than she actually was. In her portrayal of Natalie Barney as Valérie Seymour in *The Well of Loneliness*, Radclyffe Hall aptly noted how Barney's personality complemented her physical allure, giving her "a charm that lay less in physical attraction than in a great courtesy and understanding, a great will to please, a great impulse towards beauty in all its forms."[31] Throughout her life, she was appreciated for her keen wit and her sense of *bon vivant* which fitted her for her role as salon hostess.

Barney best describes her attraction to Vivien,

> a young woman who was taller than I, but who was politely bent forward in order not to appear so. She had a thin body and a charming head with straight, mousy hair, brown eyes which often sparkled with gaiety, but when her beautiful, swarthy eyelids were lowered, they revealed more than her eyes—the soul and the poetic melancholy that I sought in her. . . . Her shoulders slouched, as if they were already discouraged, her arms gestured a bit awkwardly, and her hands sometimes trembled as if they were ready to draw nearer to some invisible object which had just escaped them. . . .
>
> She had a sense of humor which was easy to restore and a childlike drollness which suddenly removed half of her twenty years. The weakness of her chin could be particularly noted in profile, but when seen from the front, no one could resist the laugh on her full lips, and her little teeth of which even the canines were not pointed. Her complexion, uniformly smooth and enhanced by a beautiful texture, was virginally pink when she became animated. Her nose was fine and slightly turned up.[32]

This description is fascinating and illuminating. For one thing, it was published in *Souvenirs indiscrets (Indiscreet Memories)* in 1960, over fifty years after Vivien's death. Despite such a long absence, Barney remembers Vivien in extraordinarily precise and minute detail. That Vivien's image was so clearly inscribed in Barney's mind despite the decades and the dozens of lovers in between is a testimony to Barney's love for her. In addition, since most of Renée Vivien's writing is quite melancholy and somber, one might suppose that the author was equally morose. The bright side of Vivien's personality is not simply wishful thinking on Barney's part, half a century after the fact. Barney's observations are confirmed by Colette: "Impossible to find anywhere in that face . . . any sign of the hidden tragic melancholy that throbs in the poetry of Renée Vivien. I never saw Renée sad."[33]

More important, however, is the underlying nature of Barney and Vivien's relationship. Barney was profoundly attracted to the poetic spirit in Vivien, whom Barney always perceived as the far more serious writer of the two. While Barney preferred living to writing, Vivien was first and foremost a poet. Barney felt Vivien had the will and talent to transform her adventures and visions into metric masterpieces. She also appreciated Vivien's potential for enjoyment and empathized with a kindred soul—

someone who would share her *joie de vivre* and her sense of fun as well as her ideals. Simultaneously attracted to the decadent, melancholy poet within, Barney managed to balance the death-driven Vivien by expanding her capability for feeling joy.

Vivien, it is clear, perceived Barney as her radiant muse, as a Beatrice who would deliciously draw her into hell as well as into paradise. She perceived Barney as a siren, tempting her toward the rocks of love on which she feared she would crash. Yet she bitterly craved Barney's love even if it meant her destruction. She also joyously participated in their escapades and adventures, which may have ironically prolonged her life, for she was never so healthy and vibrant as when she was with Barney. Furthermore, Barney's visions and fantasies, to which Vivien was so fatally drawn, expanded Vivien's thematic horizons and saved her from becoming a garden poet, extolling transitory flowers. The literary flow was not entirely in one direction. Vivien's seriousness as a poet and unusual productivity (we know that she wrote at least nine volumes of poetry, two novels, and two books of short stories in ten years) had an impact on Barney, who wrote six of her fourteen books during Vivien's lifetime, though Barney outlived her by over sixty years. Several of the books that post-dated Vivien's death, such as *Indiscreet Memories*, were also about Vivien as her memory continued to haunt Barney's imagination.

From the very beginning of their relationship, they were passionately involved with one another, so much so that when Violet Shilleto asked Vivien to visit her in the South of France in the winter of 1901, Vivien promised to go but had no intention of doing so because of her all-consuming affair with Barney. Violet Shilleto fell ill and was dying when Vivien finally arrived. Before dying, Shilleto converted to Catholicism (though her family gave her an Anglican funeral).[34] "Renée's grief for Violet was compounded by her guilt for having become estranged from her friend. She felt that she had been led to betray the friendship by this absorption in the carnal delights of [this] . . . first affair."[35] She felt torn between her "pure" love for Violet Shilleto and her "lust" for Natalie Barney. "Come to me, my two loves, my beloved. . . . / You were my splendor and my glory and my song. / You, Loreley, moonbeam of opal laughter / And you whose presence is calm and vesperal / And whose love is more pensive than the setting sun."[36]

To further intensify Vivien's agony, Barney was involved in another affair with English poet Olive Custance while Vivien sat by Violet's deathbed. In fact, Barney was constantly inconstant, while Vivien believed in traditional vows of fidelity. Their conflicting values continually strained their relationship.

Barney revealed her view on jealousy in *Cinq petits dialogues grecs [antithèses et parallèles] (Five Short Greek Dialogues [Antitheses and Parallels])*, which she published in 1902 under the masculine Greek pseudonym of "Tryphé," a choice influenced by the Greek scholar Pierre Louÿs, who was a mentor for Vivien and especially Barney. The book comprises three dialogues, two monologues, some poems, and an epilogue. In the longest dialogue, "Douces rivalités" ("Gentle Rivalries"), three women—Eranna, Ione, and Myrcles (who are apparently Violet, Renée and Natalie respectively)—debate jealousy in pseudo-Socratic style. Ione loves Myrcles but is disturbed by the latter's infidelities. Ione confesses her love and jealousy to Eranna when they are alone. Eranna also confesses to loving both Ione and Myrcles but sacrifices herself by committing suicide to unite her beloved friends. In the dialogue, at least, her tactic works.[37]

Myrcles and Eranna cite Sappho as a model to justify infidelity. As we shall see, Barney and Vivien deified Sappho and took her words as a foundation for living and writing. According to Sappho, as interpreted by Barney, infidelity should unite loves rather than separate them: "Other loves are merely like fallen flower petals in your memory. You will find in each one a fragment of yourself. My infidelities are a succession of expiatory offerings, chains of flowers binding me more closely to you."[38] For someone like Vivien, jealous by nature, it would seem more than a bit paradoxical that infidelity should be the tie that binds.

Barney and Vivien were poorly matched in other ways as well. Sexually, both liked to play the role of the suitor. Barney imagined herself to be the fearless "Amazon," pursuing women with both persistence and wiles. Obviously, they could not both be the pursuer, neither the object of desire. Furthermore, whereas Barney was free of any guilt about her sexual proclivities and about sex itself, Vivien's life and early self-inflicted death suggest that she rather did not enjoy her own body. Later in their relationship, they did seem to reach some sort of accommodation regarding Lesbian role playing, for Barney indicates in her unpublished memoirs that Vivien experienced her first orgasm in 1904 on Lesbos,[39] in some sense abdicating the role of the unfulfilled page/knight who is always in pursuit but who almost never attains sexual satisfaction. The permutations of this dynamic in their works will be discussed in a later chapter.

On the other hand, Vivien remained intensely jealous, though on some level Vivien did realize that Barney's affairs with others in no way diminished the love Barney felt for her and that her jealousy would only serve to drive Barney away. In *A Woman Appeared to Me,* Vivien tried to externalize the duality of her feelings by splitting herself into two characters: San Giovanni is the androgynous, ethereal, pure, asexual poet, and the narrator is the tormented lover of Vally or Loreley (Barney). In the novel, San Giovanni warns the narrator: "If you don't moderate your jealous rage and your wild temper, *you will lose* Vally."[40] The carnal half of Vivien was especially jealous of Barney's male suitors, even though her "poetic" self realized her fears were unfounded. San Giovanni states firmly: "She doesn't like men at all; you should know that as well as I do."[41] It is obvious that Vivien felt "split in two" by her love for Barney. One side rejected the physical attachment and was repelled by Barney's morality (or lack of it), while the other half was hopelessly attracted to her.

Despite the dual blows of Violet Shilleto's death and Barney's infidelity, Vivien's love for Barney conquered her spiritual vacillation. She considered her relationship with Barney to be predestined, inexorable, and inescapable: "Her face was the dreaded face of my Future."[42]

Although Barney and Vivien's relationship survived Shilleto's death, it declined. While most people's lives—unlike those of characters in novels—do not have beginnings, middles, and ends, the life of Renée Vivien does seem to read like a classically structured play in which the untimely death of Shilleto (early on in Act Three) provided a climax leading to an inexorable denouement. True, Vivien still experienced moments of exquisite joy with Barney and produced the bulk of her major work after Shilleto's death, yet her guilt over it, her attraction for the tranquility of death, and her determination to rejoin Shilleto grew.[43]

In the hopes of alleviating Vivien's depression, Barney took Vivien with her to Bar Harbor in the summer of 1901. They spent much of their time with Evalina Palmer. In the fall, the trio went to Bryn Mawr where Vivien and Palmer studied Greek while Barney socialized. Then Vivien went to London on the pretext of visiting her family, while Barney went to Washington, D.C. to visit hers. Barney should have been suspicious of Vivien's departure since Vivien detested England, the English, and her family, except for her sister.[44] Barney and Vivien were supposed to reunite in Paris, but after she returned there, Vivien no longer answered Barney's letters. When Barney finally arrived in Paris, Vivien refused to see her.

Barney tried without success to win back Vivien's affections and employed the wiles of her friends, including Liane de Pougy and Evalina Palmer, but Vivien adamantly refused to meet or speak with her. The situation was exacerbated by Barney and Vivien's governess, who had decided to guard Vivien from Barney and did her utmost to ensure that the two lovers would not reunite.

Barney's most imaginative attempt to recapture Vivien's attention occurred when she persuaded her friend Emma Calvé, an operatic diva, to perform an aria under Vivien's window while Barney picked up the coins that were being tossed at them from various windows by appreciative listeners. When Vivien, an ardent music lover, came out on her balcony to better hear this remarkable "street singer," Barney tossed her a bouquet of flowers encircled by a poem. Alas, the sharp-eyed governess, and not Vivien, received both the flowers and the poem and wrote Barney a sharp note warning her "to cut out the messages which are as distressing as they are useless."[45] Despite the failure of this courtly gesture, the incident elucidates the operatic level at which Barney lived, for such escapades are typically found in the pages of romances rather than in the streets of Paris.

Despite numerous checkmates by the governess, Barney was not discouraged. Shortly thereafter, Vivien went without the eagle-eyed governess to a Wagner concert near Monte Carlo. Eva Palmer agreed to attend with Vivien, but switched places with Barney in the box. Vivien seemed overjoyed to see Barney but did not show up for an appointment the next day. Instead, she sent a succinct note saying: "You can't live twice."[46]

Vivien's ambivalence may have been caused by a "morning-after" recollection of Barney's penchant for multiple relationships, a fear constantly harped on by the governess. Barney had to return quickly to Monte Carlo anyway, since she had received a telegram informing her that her father was gravely ill. By the time she reached his bedside, he had already died. After cremating him in Paris, she sailed home with Eva Palmer and Freddy Manners-Sutton.

When the trio returned to Paris, they moved into an apartment around the corner from Vivien's. Barney decided to use her newly acquired vast inheritance to redeem herself in the eyes of Vivien, who had in Barney's absence become involved with the extremely powerful Hélène, the Baroness de Zuylen de Nyevelt (née Rothschild). Barney could not comprehend how Vivien, who "had a considerable fortune, could have fallen into the golden trap."[47] The Baroness was apparently noted for having a series of mistresses, each of whom she set up with a house and a lifetime annuity after she had ended the relationship with her.[48]

Barney reestablished contact with Vivien at yet another Wagner concert, this time at Bayreuth. While the music played on, Barney read to Vivien from her prose poem *Je me souviens (I Remember)*, which was published after Vivien's death, "in the hope that she would be touched by how much [Barney] . . . had felt her loss."[49] Significantly, poetry succeeded again with Vivien where all other tactics had failed, for it was Barney's poetic talent that had initially attracted Vivien to her. This time Vivien tearfully promised to meet Barney at the end of August in Vienna where they would together take the Orient Express to Constantinople, there to embark for Lesbos.

The significance of this experience on Lesbos will be analyzed in subsequent chapters, but for now we might note that they rented two villas, and Barney suggested to Vivien that they establish a school of poetry there, as Sappho had done centuries before them. Barney and Vivien lived in the greatest happiness they had ever experienced with one another until the Baroness learned of Vivien's whereabouts and came to "reclaim her." Vivien decided to meet the Baroness in Constantinople in order to break off with her in person; instead, she was reunited with the Baroness and did not meet Barney in Paris as they had planned.

Despite the failure of Barney's enterprise, the conception was a unique and courageous one. It was unthinkable for two young, single, unaccompanied women to go to such a strange country, not merely to escape from society's distaste for and persecution of Lesbians,[50] but to create a positive poetic environment as well. As we shall see, many of Barney's other ideas also worked better in theory than in practice. This failed experiment, however, was significant in that it planted the seeds that would bloom into Barney's Academy of Women over two decades later in 1927.

The second rupture with Vivien was the final one, yet the years that Vivien had spent with Barney had been extremely productive for both writers. Vivien wrote and published eight books. In addition to expansions on Sapphic fragments in *Sapho (Sappho)*, 1903, and *Les Kitharèdes (The Kitharedes)*, 1904, Vivien produced four volumes of poetry: *Etudes et préludes (Etudes and Preludes)*, 1901; *Cendres et poussières (Ashes and Dust)*, 1902; *Evocations*, 1903; and *La Vénus des aveugles (The Venus of the Blind)*, 1904. The authorship of her first book was attributed to "R. Vivien," and she signed cards accompanying review copies sent to critics with a male given name, "René." In 1903, she used the feminine name "Renée" for the first time on the cover of *Evocations*; some scandal ensued when it was discovered that the author of these passionate poems

to women was also female. As is simple to deduce, René[e] means "reborn" in French, and Vivien probably refers to Viviane, the Lady of the
Lake, a figure from the courtly romances she so much admired.

All four volumes of poetry consisted primarily of love sonnets, most of
them to Barney and Shilleto. Barney is referred to by many names,
including Atthis (Sappho's friend) and Loreley, but she is also simply "the
blond one" and lilies. Beginning in *Evocations*, Barney is often referred to
in the past tense, as in "I once loved you, Atthis!"[51] This poem probably
represents their first rupture. Violet Shilleto is usually called Ione, but
she is also referred to as Timas (another of Sappho's followers, who died a
virgin). In both the poems and *A Woman Appeared to Me* she is represented by violets. The poems to Violet decry her untimely death. Eva
Palmer in both Vivien's poems and in *A Woman Appeared to Me* is often
referred to as the goddess of autumn or as the sunset, perhaps because of
her flaming red hair.

During her relationship with Barney, Vivien also began writing prose
poems and tales. The first volume, published in 1902, was entitled
Brumes de fjords (Fogs of the Fjords). Several of the tales reflect Vivien's
sense of feeling torn by different loves but ultimately wishing to follow
the "pure" life of a poet. For example, in "Les Vents" ("The Winds"), the
narrator meets the four winds who try to tempt her in different directions. She refuses each temptation by replying: "My soul is detained in
the village by the uncertain smile of a virgin."[52] This theme is recast in
another tale, "Les Deux amours" ("The Two Loves"), in which the protagonist cannot choose between his wife and his yearning for the kingdom of the dead. In the end he is told that he is one of those "who don't
know how to choose, one of those who hesitate eternally."[53] Such was
Vivien's own quandary—being unable to choose between loving Barney or
the Baroness and following Shilleto into the shadowy world of the dead.

Many of the stories here, and also in her 1904 collection of short stories
La Dame à la louve (The Woman of the Wolf), rewrite myth and folklore,
and these will be further discussed later. In addition to the content, *Fogs
of the Fjords* is Vivien's first work in which the dedication "to my Friend,
H.L.C.B." appears. Most critics agree that the initials stand for "Hélène-
Louise-Charlotte-Bettina"—the weighty first names of the Baroness de
Zuylen de Nyevelt. The dedication, repeated in later volumes, indicates
that the Baroness was a source of literary inspiration to Vivien, although
it is unclear whether she acted as muse, financial patroness of the arts, or
as both. Ironically, she does not appear in Vivien's works as the thinly
disguised subject of poems or stories, as Barney and Shilleto so clearly do.

Some critics, including Paul Lorenz, Jean-Paul Goujon, Jeanne Manning, Gayle Rubin, and George Wickes, feel that the Baroness might have played another role—that of co-author with Vivien of several books under the name of Paule Riversdale. Lorenz supports his theory by pointing out that Vivien's real first name is Pauline. As for Riversdale, Lorenz explains: "Riversdale in English means the vale around a river or the river of a vale. Then one can ask oneself whether this river does not empty itself in the little mountain lake or tarn, which the English name of the poet signifies."[54]

This evidence does not seem overwhelming. For one thing, it does not explain how this name contains the Baroness as co-author. Nor does it explain why Vivien would choose another *nom de plume* to write books of essentially the same nature. Furthermore, the "vale" which Lorenz takes to signify "Tarn" might equally well signify "Vally," one of the names Vivien used for Barney in the novel *A Woman Appeared to Me.* Most striking, however, are the stylistic differences between the Baroness and Renée Vivien. The Baroness de Zuylen de Nyevelt did pen and publish several novels, including *L'Enjoleuse (The Wily Lady)*, *L'Impossible sincerité (The Impossible Sincerity)*, and *La Dernière étreinte (The Last Embrace)*. She also wrote a book of poetry, *Effeuillements* (a pun meaning *The Shedding of Leaves* or *Striptease*). The first two are primarily drawing room romances and show no similarity of style with either Renée Vivien or Paule Riversdale. Her poetry lacks commitment and passion. Her verse is timid and bland when compared to Vivien's. Almost all her poems are in quatrains with an ABBA rhyme scheme whereas Vivien preferred the sonnet. Perhaps she feared damaging the reputation of the noble families to which she was connected by both birth and marriage, but to put it rather bluntly, her writing is vastly inferior. It simply does not seem possible that she was secretly half of Paule Riversdale.

The few hard facts about the relationship between Vivien and Riversdale remain puzzling. There are two firm pieces of evidence. In August 1903, Vivien wrote to Charles-Brun, "I am here with Paule Riversdale."[55] Simone Burgues, the niece of Charles-Brun, has taken this to mean, "I am working on the book which will be signed Riversdale,"[56] which at that time would have been *L'Etre double (Double Being)*. But how could Vivien be *with* Paule Riversdale if she *were* Paule Riversdale, unless she were quite schizophrenic, which is not among Vivien's known ailments. More convincingly, however, Vivien used the name Riversdale to sign a humorous Christmas card to Charles-Brun. According to Burgues, the handwriting "imitated—though distantly—that of Hélène de Zuylen. But it was surely hers [Vivien's]."[57] This time the card was clearly a prank; Vivien was either recognizing an affinity between her style and that of Riversdale, or she was indicating that the Baroness was Riversdale, or perhaps that she herself was Riversdale.

At this point in time, the mystery of Riversdale's identity cannot be lifted with any certainty. Though the Bibliothèque Nationale in Paris lists Riversdale as the pseudonym of Vivien and de Zuylen de Nyevelt, I am unconvinced of the probability of this literary collaboration. With these caveats in mind, I will discuss one work of Riversdale, which is thematically similar to those of Vivien and Barney.

In any case, after 1904, the Baroness replaced Barney (although there is some evidence that she too disappeared from Vivien's life after 1905). After her final separation from Barney, Vivien went in two opposite directions, the combination of which hastened her death. On one hand, in true Rimbaudian fashion, she spent part of her time as a restless traveler, voyaging to the Middle East, the Mediterranean, the Orient, and back to Lesbos. She spent the rest of her time in Paris in a dark, airless, gloomy apartment at 23, avenue du Bois, which she filled with Oriental *objets d'art* and Buddhas that she had acquired on her journeys. Her Parisian apartment is best described by Colette, who lived in the next building, which adjoined Vivien's through the courtyard:

> The vast, dark, sumptuous, and ever-changing flat in the avenue du Bois . . . has never been well-described, by the way. Except for some gigantic Buddhas, all the furnishings moved mysteriously; after provoking surprise and admiration for a time, they had a way of disappearing. . . . [sic]
>
> Among the unstable marvels, Renée wandered, not so much clad as veiled in black or purple, almost invisible in the scented darkness of the immense rooms barricaded with leaded windows, the air heavy with curtains and incense. . . .
>
> The first time I dined at her place, three brown tapers dripped waxen tears in tall candlesticks and did not dispel the gloom. A low table, from the Orient, offered a pell-mell assortment of *les hors d'oeuvre*. . . .[58]

Colette also reports that Vivien barely touched her food but drank quantities of Greek, Russian, and Oriental alcohol. Apparently, several times at the beginning or in the middle of the meal, Vivien would leave her dinner guests because an unnamed lover would command her presence. Once, she whispered to Colette, "Hush, I'm requisitioned. *She* is terrible at present."[59] On another occasion, "she did not finish what she had to say but burst into tears and fled. A carriage waiting for her outside bore her away."[60] The unidentified woman was perhaps the Baroness, but if Colette did see and recognize her, she remains discreet about the identity of Vivien's mysterious lover. No matter who the mystery lady was, Vivien was no longer the young poet Colette had never seen unhappy.

Vivien's self-abuse eventually took its toll, and her death wish was fulfilled. From most accounts, her condition gradually declined over a period of years, and she died on 18 November 1909, and was buried at Passy Graveyard in Paris. The cause of her death is unclear. Colette's version has led most critics to believe that she died of alcoholism or anorexia, perhaps a combination of both. Pneumonia may have been the direct cause of death.

Colette relates one story that portrays Vivien's illness as a classic case of anorexia, then unrecognized as a disease. Vivien had decided that she was ten pounds too heavy to play the role of Jane Grey in a *tableau vivant*. She fasted for ten days and lost ten pounds. After the play, Vivien fainted backstage.[61] As Sandra Gilbert and Susan Gubar demonstrated in their germinal study of women writers in the nineteenth century, *The Madwoman in the Attic*, anorexia was too often the fate of the rebellious woman writer or of her heroines. Though Vivien's death came a decade after the nineteenth century had drawn to a close, she was almost entirely a product of the Victorian era. Colette's account shows that Vivien irrationally considered herself obese. She also felt a great loathing of pregnancy and reproduction, and anorexia often psychologically represents a fear of impregnation.[62] Ironically, she "confined" herself in a way much stricter and crueller than physical pregnancy would have done. But more cogently, her self-starvation was her ultimate rebellion against the patriarchy. Like Caroline Helstone's anorexia in Charlotte Brontë's *Shirley*, Vivien's

> self-starvation is also a rejection of what her society has defined as nourishing. As an act of revolt, . . . fasting is a refusal to feed on foreign foods. Since eating maintains the self, in a discredited world it is a compromise implying acquiescence. Women will starve in silence, [as] Brontë [also] seems to imply, until new stories are created that confer upon them the power of naming themselves and controlling their world.[63]

Specifically in Vivien's case, her imbibing only exotic alcohol and foodstuffs indicated an unwillingness to conform to the norm—what was considered "acceptable." She went to her death defiantly abnormal, down to her choice of nourishment.

An early death was certainly in keeping with Vivien's constant cult of

death. After all, according to legend, her idol, Sappho, committed suicide
(though Sappho was middle-aged by then). As Barney noted, "This poetess
fed on legends of her [Sappho's] island where great love can only culmi-
nate in death. How could she have contented herself with passions that
would only end in fulfillment?"[64]

It seems a contradiction that Vivien's apparent suicidal anorexic behavior goes hand in hand with so many stories about her deathbed
conversion to Catholicism, a religion which considers such a death to be a
mortal sin. Yet, biographers such as André Germain and Yves-Gérard Le
Dantec emphasize the story, perhaps to prove that Vivien is worthy of our
consideration as a poet. Germain even stresses that Vivien tried to rally
but she was too weak.[65] On the other hand, Natalie Barney, who was a
pagan to the end, believed at first that if Vivien converted, the act had to
be only a momentary lapse.

Barney expressed her bitter feelings about the "trumped-up conversion"
in one of her many poems on Renée Vivien's death. She begins the poem
by citing a line of Vivien's from *A l'heure des mains jointes (At the Hour
of Joined Hands):* "O, Christ, I don't know thee."[66] Then Barney expands
on it with a poem of lamentation and revenge:

> . . . Et pourtant ils ont pris ton âme splenétique
> Aux décédants espoirs du dogme catholique,
> Voulant ouvrir tes yeux avides de repos
> A leur éternité. . . .
> Et la petite nuit de tes belles paupières
> Te donneras l'oubli des prêtres, des prières:
> Tes esprits affaiblis, ils purent te changer
> Mais l'œuvre de ta vie est là pour te venger.
> Ils ont caché ton corps païen sous une pierre
> Chrétienne, ton squelette émiette sa poussière.

> . . . And nevertheless they have delivered your
>   splenetic soul
> To the deathbed hopes of Catholic dogma,
> Hoping to open your eyes so avid for rest
> To their eternity. . . .
> But one brief night on your beautiful eyelids
> Will make you forget the priests, the prayers:
> Your weakened spirits, they could change you
> But the work of your life is there to avenge you.
> They have hidden your pagan body under a Christian
> Stone, your skeleton is crumbling into dust.[67]

Years later, Barney modified her views and saw Vivien's Catholicism as a natural outcome of her beliefs:

> Born Protestant (people don't convert to Protestantism), she became Catholic, and the priest who had converted her childhood friend [Violet] gave her "the consolation that the priest comes to give."
>
>   . . . But it isn't necessary to say that Renée Vivien "converted"; rather, all her life had been an *evolution* towards this final and undeniable hope.[68]

Barney, who had rarely seen Vivien in years, obviously could not have witnessed the latter's conversion. She did hear of Vivien's illness and rushed to her house but arrived too late. She was told in a matter-of-fact tone that Vivien had just died. She expressed her reaction in a poem, "La Chambre vide" ("The Empty Room"): " 'Too late?' This spectral word / To warn me? / Midnight sounds, I'm cold, I fear / Dying."[69] It was one of the few times that Barney would express any fear or negative feelings about death. Neither did she long to follow Vivien, for the cult of death was one issue on which Barney and Vivien did not even faintly agree. Barney enjoyed living to the fullest and generally did not contemplate death. Nor did she mourn those who had died or even (with few exceptions) attend their funerals. In this instance, Barney did mourn her lover while simultaneously realizing that Vivien died precisely the death she had craved, that she was a martyr of beauty, and that she would now join Marlowe, Villon, and especially Keats, poets who had also died young.[70]

Despite the insistence of Barney's housekeeper, Berthe Cleyrergue, that Barney only loved Romaine Brooks,[71] Barney left a number of poems attesting to her love for Vivien, and to missing her, such as the following verse: "Atthis, for whom in your verses you are gently sorry / Is faithful to the memory of which nothing is illusion / And wishes to follow you, wearing amulets on her neck. . . ."[72]

The source of these lines is *Actes et entr'actes (Acts and Entr'acts)*, one of several works that can be directly linked to Barney's relationship with Vivien. Published in 1910, this work is a collection of poems and plays in verse. Many of the poems deal with Barney's feelings about Vivien's untimely death. One play, "La Double mort" ("Double Death"), is a parable about her feelings of loss. In it, Bertrand and Gaspard, former lovers of Faustine, both grieve for her after she has died. Bertrand curses traditional religion and Faustine's conversion to it. After Faustine's death, he fights with Gaspard for possession of her locket, since each expects to find his own portrait within. Instead, they find the portrait of a priest. In other words, Faustine was lost to a belief, not another lover, as perhaps Barney lost Vivien to her poetry or religion or thirst for death, rather than to the Baroness or a subsequent lover. The choice of the name "Faustine" for the departed heroine is also intriguing, perhaps suggesting that Vivien, in either her writing or her pursuit of both Catholicism and Eastern religions, was seeking forbidden knowledge and/or the unknowable. The priest in the play saves Faustine's soul not from a pact with a devil but from love.[73]

Acts and Entr'acts, Five Short Greek Dialogues, and *I Remember* are the books by Natalie Barney on which Renée Vivien had the most direct influence, although the themes and ideas they explored together would endure in Barney's later work. *I Remember*, already briefly mentioned, is a prose poem, in which Barney reflected on her relationship with Renée Vivien, after their first rupture. In 1910 Barney also published her first book of *pensées* ("thoughts"), as she would later call them, though this volume was entitled *Eparpillements (Scatterings)*. This title, though facetious, is an apt one, for the *pensées* are not in the tradition of Pascal, but of La Rochefoucauld. They are primarily maxims and bons mots without the extreme seriousness of purpose one would associate with Pascal nor the in-depth description of characters one would associate with La Bruyère. *Scatterings*, like the two books of *pensées* by Barney, contains fragments of unfinished thoughts as well as of unfinished novels. She seemed to pride herself on displaying what she hadn't taken the time or energy to complete.

Before examining Barney's life after the death of Vivien, let us briefly explore Vivien's works written after her separation from Barney. As previously mentioned, Vivien penned her version of her affair with Barney in a Symbolist novel, *A Woman Appeared to Me*. She also wrote six more volumes of poetry, three of which were published after her death: *At the Hour of Joined Hands, Sillages (Wakes), Flambeaux éteints (Extinguished Torches), Dans un coin de violettes (In a Corner of Violets), Les Vents des vaisseaux (The Winds of the Vessels)*, and *Haillons (Rags)*.

In short, the relationship stimulated the literary production of both women though neither writer ever established a place for herself in the canon of premier women writers. Their love, however, loomed larger than their work: Their doomed romance has been commonly known in Lesbian/feminist communities in North America and Europe while their books remain largely unread and untranslated, except for four volumes by Vivien. In some ways they were dreadfully mismatched: The unapologetic, lusty Barney was hopelessly drawn to the anorexic, androgynous Vivien, who was quite uncomfortable with her own body and its sexual drives. Yet, despite their limitations, they enacted their romance on an operatic scale and on a global stage stretching from Bar Harbor to Lesbos. For this great love they are justly remembered, for they openly transgressed the rules of family and convention before the word *Lesbian* was even in use.

II.

STAYING ON, BUT NEVER ALONE

In 1909, the year Vivien died, Natalie Clifford Barney moved to 20, rue Jacob, where she would reside for over half a century. "The most distinctive feature of the property she rented is a small Doric temple tucked away in a corner of the garden. . . . The inscription on its pediment dedicates the temple *à l'amitié*, 'to friendship,' and official records show that it dates back only to the early nineteenth century."[1]

Barney opened a salon in October of 1909; in good weather, theatricals and other events were held in her garden. Such events were not new to Barney. Her own mother, Alice Pike Barney, had staged similar amusements at the family home in Washington, D.C. At her previous residence, Barney had staged theatricals, which included Colette and Mata Hari, among others. She had also attended salons run by others, at which she was introduced to the much sought-after Count Robert de Montesquiou. When she opened her own salon, he became a devotee, as did Lucie Delarue-Mardrus, and J. C. Mardrus, with both of whom she had been intimate friends for years. Both Mardruses were writers: Joseph-Charles Mardrus had translated *The Arabian Nights* into French, and these tales had a great influence on both Barney and Vivien. Lucie was the author of several novels, including *L'Ange et les pervers (The Angel and the Perverts)*, written in 1930, about her Lesbian relationship with Natalie Barney. She also wrote a book of poems called *Nos secrètes amours (Our Secret Loves)*, a title which Barney later borrowed for her unpublished memoirs.

Another important habitué of the salon was Elisabeth de Gramont, the Duchess de Clermont-Tonnerre, another lifelong friend of Natalie's. She authored four volumes of memoirs of the era, the first of which was entitled *Au temps des équipages (In the Era of Carriages)*. Two other important regulars were Natalie's tutor, Charles-Brun, and Pierre Louÿs, author of *Songs of Bilitis* and *Aphrodite*.

The salon was open every Friday, and one great person brought another. Visitors to the salon included André Gide, Paul Valéry, Paul Claudel, Jean Cocteau, Gabriele d'Annunzio, Anatole France, Auguste Rodin, Rabindranath Tagore, James Joyce, Rainer-Maria Rilke, Isadora Duncan, Gertrude Stein, Salomon Reinach, André Germain, Edmond Jaloux, André Rouveyre, Oscar Milosz, and Max Jacob. Many of those mentioned here were "regulars," and almost every great intellectual in Europe visited 20, rue Jacob at one time or another. The attendees were primarily writers and scholars, though Barney also knew artists such as José de Charmoy and Auguste Rodin. In general, though, the artists tended to frequent Gertrude Stein's salon. Stein herself went on rare occasions to Barney's house, especially later when Barney formed the Academy of Women. Barney wrote character sketches of some of her famous salon attendees in *Aventures de l'esprit (Adventures of the Mind)* in 1929 and *Traits et portraits (Traits and Portraits)* in 1963.

What made Barney the perfect hostess as well as the perfect pro-priestess of the Temple of Friendship is that, above all, she prized cama-raderie. Although she did not like everyone—especially the common, unintellectual person—she was a loyal friend to many men and women. One of her most widely repeated remarks is about friendship: "I am very lazy; once I confer friendship, I never take it back."[2] She once defined friendship as a "pact above passions, the only indissoluble marriage both by logic and excellence. Like the snail's shell, . . . friendship grows a new layer each year. . . ."[3] Friendship is a theme of two of her major works, *Pensées d'une amazone (Thoughts of an Amazon)*, written in 1920 and *Nouvelles pensées de l'amazone (More Thoughts of the Amazon)*, written in 1939, as well as of her memoirs.

In promoting Barney's titillating affairs with so many famous women, biographers such as Jean Chalon and George Wickes, as well as Gayle Rubin in her slide presentation on Barney, tend to downplay (perhaps inadvertently) this nonsexual side of Barney's liaisons. Ironically, while intending to create "hagiography," as Rubin termed her portrayal of Barney's gallery of lovers,[4] such biography is ultimately reductionist, for it caricatures Barney as a mindless Dona Juana, which was how Djuna Barnes also portrayed her in her *Ladies Almanack*, where Barnes transformed Barney into the insatiable Dame Evangeline Musset. As we shall see, Barney disdained sexuality merely for the sake of carnal enjoyment, a point which brought her into contention with male homosexuals, such as Gide. While her taste in lovers seems justly praised, we should comprehend that her affairs led to, expressed, or consummated a friendship: They were not the goals, but the means.

She was, by her own definition, the Amazon of friendship,[5] a name she acquired from Remy de Gourmont, surely one of her greatest friends and admirers. Gourmont was a widely read columnist for the *Mercure de France* and the author of several books. André Rouveyre, who wrote two books about Gourmont, described him with apparent adoration: "He had an encyclopedic mind. . . . He had a vast grasp of culture, an insatiable curiosity, and an Epicurean philosophy which included everything. His individual genius lay in his delightful style. . . . He thought and he wrote with clarity."[6]

It is easy to see why Barney, who had very far-reaching interests, was attracted to Gourmont's Renaissance mind. Furthermore, Barney, who loved pleasure above all else, empathized with his Epicureanism. Ironically, by the time Barney had met him in 1910, Gourmont had long been forced to abandon his own sensual bent. Chronically and severely afflicted by lupus, which made him quite hideous, he shut himself up in his apartment. Undeterred as always by a reluctant conquest, Barney courted him with flowers, until she finally broke down his resistance and ended his seclusion. After their friendship had flowered, she became the only one who could entice him to leave his apartment for a walk in the Bois de Boulogne or for an excursion on a boat.

Barney appealed to his sense of higher, courtly love. He liked to live out passions and adventures in his mind in the way Barney sought to actualize hers. They were kindred spirits. Though Gourmont was passionately in love with her, the relationship remained emotional rather than physical due to Barney's Lesbianism and Gourmont's affliction. "Miss Barney, fiercely beautiful, capricious, and witty, treated Remy de Gourmont in a novel enough way to awaken in him his paradoxical composition and give him a sort of ultimate ecstasy. She was an infernal Beatrice to whom Remy de Gourmont went each day to open up the arcana of his sensual knowledge and to exude his love."[7]

Later Rouveyre accused Barney of consciously making Gourmont fall in love with her to a tortuous extent. "The fact remains that, physically indifferent but enveloped by his wisdom, Barney would esteem Gourmont in order to feed off his restless mind. At the same time, the richest mind of this generation adored her, to the point of crucifixion. And she was successful at it."[8]

It can be conceded that although Gourmont outwardly accepted the "platonic" terms of the relationship dictated to him by Barney—after all, he had no choice—inwardly he burned with passion. As Rouveyre notes in his book, Barney would have to be extremely naive to claim, as she did, that she never noticed it. Once, when she had withdrawn in anger the hand she usually permitted him to hold, he was so upset that he spent a sleepless night and fretted over it the next day. He then wrote her: "I love you with so much fear and such a feeling of unworthiness that my desire can only be manifested in a timid tenderness, the tenderness of a sick person, the tenderness of a desperate person. Oh! Don't withdraw those hands, the only part of you I dare to wish for."[9]

Surely these are the words of a man desperately in love (or a *précieux!*), but he managed to keep his distance in order to preserve whatever relationship he did have. In all his letters to her, he uses the intimate French form of *you ("tu")* only once, and in the very next paragraph he returns to *vous*.[10] His words reveal a man who approached love in a courtly, subservient way: He pursued her while understanding that she was unattainable.[11] If there was one thing Barney was perfectly clear about, it was her sexual proclivities, and there is no need to suppose that Barney "led him on," or had a "will like Nero's" as Rouveyre asserts.[12] She loved Gourmont for his intellect and made the terms of the relationship clear. Gourmont accepted.

Having grown up in privileged circumstances that allowed her to avoid marriage and/or employment and having managed to surround herself in her salon with the great men of her time, Barney had somehow sheltered herself from—or chose to ignore—the typical dynamics of male/female relationships. In the milieu of the salon, where most of her encounters with men transpired, she was protected from the ardor of men by the size of the gatherings, which discouraged intimacy and precluded *tête-à-tête* encounters. On her own turf, she believed (or hoped) that men would accept her as a witty, inspired intellectual as well as a generous and habile hostess. In general, her male guests do seem to have behaved courteously, with some exceptions. William Carlos Williams relates an anecdote about a member of the Chamber of Deputies who became so incensed at the sight of women dancing together that he "took out his tool and, shaking it right and left, yelled out in a rage, 'Have you never seen one of these?' "[13] It should also be mentioned that quite a few of the men who attended Barney's salon were homosexual; therefore, physical attraction was not an issue for them.

Due to Gourmont's lupus, Barney visited him in his house, an act which in itself is considered a sexual invitation in patriarchal culture. She did not see—or chose to not see—that despite her avowed Lesbianism, Gourmont would still see her primarily as a female object of desire and as a source of inspiration, not as a simpatico companion nor as an intellectual equal. His condescension becomes evident when we recall the manner in which he thrust the title of "Amazon" on her without consulting her: "For you are the Amazon, and you will remain the Amazon so long as it doesn't bore you, and perhaps even after that, in the ashes of my heart."[14] Fortunately, she embraced the title, which referred to her habit of wearing a riding costume (*en amazone* in French), but it is evident that had she objected, Gourmont would have felt it his artistic right to call her what he wished.

Indeed, his two books about her cast her into the traditional female role of muse. She is treated not as an equal, but as a witty, Amazonian Beatrice, inspiring Gourmont to create glorious tributes to her. He never perceived her as she really was but as he imagined and wanted her to be. He confessed this to her in a personal letter, which was posthumously published in *Intimate Letters to the Amazon* (1926): "To everyone, I answer that it [*Letters to the Amazon*] is pure fiction and that the Amazon is a creature of my imagination. Perhaps it's true in part, since we always recreate the people we love in order to love them."[15]

Gourmont died in 1915, but he left behind a curious public demanding to hear directly from the Amazon who had inspired such letters and ideas. And so Barney gave them her own views on chastity, friendship, morality, love, religion, and other topics in *Thoughts of an Amazon* and later in *More Thoughts of the Amazon*. Interestingly enough, Barney, who prided herself on her indiscretion, never published the letters she had written to Gourmont.

Gourmont died after the outbreak of World War I, a war Natalie Barney opposed. Her mother and sister were also ardent pacifists. Alice Pike Barney was president of her local branch of the Women's Peace Party.[16] Laura Dreyfus-Barney was a member of the International Women's Council and represented them at the League of Nations. In a remarkable speech she made in 1925 before the Los Angeles City Club, she asserted:

> "We must make the youth of the world realize that the moral code of the individual must be applied to the relations between nations. Theft, attack, rapine, all the crimes for which the laws of a nation penalize the individual, must be handled in an identical manner by a court or arbitration, world court, league of nations, or what you will.

"Once we have made the youth of the world realize this fundamental premise, we shall have taken the first, tremendous step to end war and all its miseries."[17]

Her feminist perspective that there is a deep-rooted connection between war and male aggression against the individual was unique then, though many male pacifists today still deny such an analogy.

Natalie Barney shared the ideals of her mother and sister. In 1917 she held anti-war meetings on the steps of the Temple of Friendship. Like Laura, she laid the blame for war at the feet of men. "War—this child men give birth to—they father death as women mother life, with courage and without choice."[18] Like Laura, Natalie believed that "war represents an extreme form of male aggression," but Shari Benstock exaggerates Natalie Barney's feminist consciousness when she claims that this murderous behavior is "apparent in all male relationships."[19] For someone who loved life and pleasure as much as Natalie Barney did, war was simply the unthinkable antithesis: "Those who *love* war lack the love of an adequate sport—the art of living."[20] Thus, though Laura and Natalie Barney were among the first to connect rape and war, war and machismo, Natalie Barney did not blame all men, only those who did not fully appreciate the real pleasures of life.

Barney remained in France throughout the war. When things became too difficult in Paris, she left and went to stay at Honfleur with Lucie Delarue-Mardrus, who was now divorced. Barney refused to return to the United States. Although she opposed the war philosophically, she did side with the French and condemn the Germans. After all, she felt the French shared her taste for the good life. "I do not believe that the French lack perspicacity; rather, they are incapable of becoming bored. And to think about and prepare for war is boring, boring for everyone. It's being locked in barracks."[21] The war was surely the fault of the Germans: "In Germany, they've even militarized their forests. . . ."[22]

Many of Barney's friends did not share her opinions. The Duchess de Clermont-Tonnerre joined the Red Cross, as did Lucie Delarue-Mardrus and many American and British citizens in Paris, such as Gertrude Stein, Alice B. Toklas, and Radclyffe Hall. Ironically, Barney met and fell in love with one of the women who supported the war: Romaine Brooks.

Natalie Barney probably met Romaine Brooks on the eve of the war, although the exact date is not agreed upon by their biographers. Romaine Brooks had followed a similar path to Paris. Though hardly anyone was as rich as Barney, Brooks came from an extremely wealthy family, the Goddards. Her father abandoned her mother shortly after Beatrice Romaine Goddard was born on 1 May 1874 in Rome. Her childhood was an unpleasant memory for her because her mother treated her like a servant and preferred her sickly brother, Henry St. Mar. At one point, according to Brooks, Mrs. Goddard gave her daughter—temporarily, at least—to be raised by a charwoman. Although Mrs. Goddard reluctantly retrieved her daughter, primarily to care for the unmanageable St. Mar, Romaine never forgave the insult to her self-worth. In 1895, Romaine made her way to Paris in order to study music and to escape from her family. From there she went to Rome and Capri to study painting. St. Mar died, and her mother was forced to settle her estate on Romaine and her sister, Maya. Romaine then briefly married homosexual pianist John Brooks, who had befriended her in her days of dire poverty when her mother allotted her only 300 francs per month. Romaine later settled 300 pounds per month on him and decided to move to Paris without him, though she retained his name. She returned to Paris in 1905 and began painting portraits, which became her forte.

Feminists with a Freudian bent might make much of the fact that both Alice Pike Barney and Romaine Brooks were portrait painters who had been influenced by Whistler (though there is no direct evidence that Brooks actually studied with him).[23] Like Whistler, Brooks used subdued colors and framed her figures in grey and black. She was called the "thief of souls,"[24] for she painted people as they were, not as they appeared. Natalie Barney reported that one of Brooks's models complained, "You haven't beautified me!" to which Brooks replied, "I have ennobled you."[25] Other clients were apparently so dissatisfied with the appearance of their souls that they refused to pay for the portraits they had commissioned.

Brooks's personal wealth and the lack of necessity to sell any of her work protected her from the criticism of her peers. If a client refused to pay for the work she had commissioned, it mattered little to Brooks, who didn't like to part with paintings anyway, and who even went so far as to buy back paintings she had given to Robert de Montesquiou. Her financial independence allowed her to become complacent with whatever subjects and style pleased her, rather than to strive to better herself to achieve sales in a competitive art market and foster a growing reputation with critics.

Barney, as one might expect, defended Brooks's portraits as honest and almost above reproach: "Almost subconsciously psychological, she puts on her canvases the best hidden secrets of the individuals she paints. She extracts their essence, relieves them of the pains of existence by such a strong and delicate avowal of who they are that they themselves gain something from it."[26]

Brooks painted some of the habitués of Barney's salon, including the Duchess de Clermont-Tonnerre. Brooks's portrayal of the members of Barney's salon is selective, and it is interesting to note which members she chose to portray and which members she neglected, and why. While the salon provided an array of subjects, Brooks was uncomfortable painting her major rivals for Barney's affection. Unlike Alice Pike Barney, Brooks had a personal stake in the level of competition a rival presented. Natalie would have been offended had Brooks created a cruel portrait of one of her lovers or demi-liaisons, while she did not seem to object to the apparent cruelty of the portrait of Lady Una Troubridge. Therefore, Brooks wisely chose to avoid portraying any of her salient rivals, such as Dolly Wilde, who had a major affair with Barney in the 1920s and 1930s, until Wilde was finally banished from Barney's affection by Brooks's jealousy. Another missing portrait would be that of Nadine Wong, who held a major place in Barney's affections until World War II called her back to China.

Brooks also painted Natalie Barney by herself as the Amazon. The portrait is oddly soft for Brooks and is perhaps veiled with love. Wrapped in a fur coat, Barney looks out at us. On a table to her left is a statue of a rearing horse, representing Barney's spirit as well as her nickname. As Shari Benstock notes, "Only Natalie is spared a hard, tight-lipped and angry mouth; only Natalie is given eyes that are dark and soft rather than small and piercing."[27]

Brooks's best work, in my opinion, is her self-portrait. Wearing a black coat and top hat, Brooks stares directly at the viewer from under the brim of her hat. There is a second set of eyes under the hatband (unnoticeable in reproductions of the painting)—perhaps suggestive of the inner vision of the artist. Behind Brooks is the outline of a city in ruins.[28]

As might be expected, Brooks and Barney greatly influenced one another's works. During their happiest years, Brooks's line drawings in particular took on a humorous quality, one not noted by her biographer, Meryle Secrest, who depicts Brooks as an extremely unhappy person.[29] In fact, all the commentaries on Brooks, including Benstock's, accept the dour stereotype of her and totally overlook the humor so apparent in her sketches. In Brooks's drawing "Life," for example, a central figure is surrounded by many heads and arms of different sizes—all touching her. At her feet is curled an infant in a fetal position. In the space under the woman's left arm a monkey peers out, adding a humorous touch to the grouping. In other drawings Brooks makes wry visual commentaries on such issues as "Enemy Fat."[30]

Brooks and Barney collaborated on a novel entitled *The One Who Is Legion, Or A.D.'s After-Life*, which was privately printed in London in 1930. It contains two illustrations of androgynous skeletal figures by Romaine Brooks. Aside from "The Woman Who Lives with Me" (which was an anonymous, undated pamphlet, but which was probably written around 1905), *The One Who Is Legion* is Barney's only major work in English. She did write a number of English-language plays, including "The Color of His Soul" (co-authored by Alice Pike Barney) and "Brothers in Arms," but these were never produced or published. The theme of *The One Who Is Legion* is androgyny, which will be discussed in a later chapter.

The One Who Is Legion is Barney's last major work, except for *More Thoughts of the Amazon*, which has already been discussed. After 1940, when she was over sixty years old, Barney published memoirs and portraits of friends, including *Traits and Portraits*, *Adventures of the Mind*, and *Indiscreet Memories*, most of which appeared earlier in journals. To some degree, she portrayed her acquaintances with her pen and ink as Brooks did with acrylic and brush. Though Barney's portraits were somewhat kinder, they were no less honest or less shrewd in their appraisal.

Barney's relationship with Brooks was her longest—over fifty years—but they experienced some of the same difficulties that Barney had had with Vivien. Barney had the misfortune to be attracted to women who were Lesbians but who were otherwise conventional. The only exception was Dolly Wilde, who, like her famous uncle Oscar, did not care for the tyranny of the majority. In fact, Dolly liked to say that she had become more "Oscar-like than Oscar was like himself."[31] (She also apparently inherited his wit.) Brooks, on the other hand, like Vivien, was essentially monogamous, and Barney, as usual, was not. Brooks never accepted Barney's other lovers and finally drove Dolly Wilde away by giving Barney an ultimatum. Except for Dolly Wilde, Barney seemed never to find women who shared what she considered to be her Sapphic ideal of multiple relationships without jealousy. Even if her lovers (for example, Renée Vivien) tried to agree with her in principle, Barney's practice of infidelity brought out the most traditional responses of rage and jealousy. In fact, when Barney and Brooks finally separated in their eighties—with Brooks so bitter that she refused to see Barney ever again—it was over Barney's affair with another woman, Janine Lahovary.

Meanwhile, after World War I, Barney and Brooks returned to Paris. In 1927, Barney gathered the women who had been united in her antiwar drive and founded the Academy of Women, a counterpart to the Académie Française, which finally admitted a token woman in 1980. "Most of the time Natalie had no planned program for the salon but merely a weekly gathering of invited guests and the habitués who had a standing invitation. But in 1927 she made a concerted effort to organize a series of special meetings featuring women writers."[32] Among those who appeared at the Academy of Women were Aurel (originally a rare enemy of Barney's, but with whom there had been a reconciliation in 1917 due to their common antiwar sentiment), Lucie Delarue-Mardrus, Colette, Gertrude Stein, Mina Loy, Rachilde, and Elisabeth de Gramont, the Duchess de Clermont-Tonnerre. "There were also 'retrospectives' on the work of Renée Vivien and Marie Lénéru."[33]

The Academy of Women must be regarded as one of Barney's most salient achievements. For one thing, it was one of the first efforts to organize women writers. In some ways it was the natural outgrowth of what Barney had been striving for throughout her life, with her plays and *tableaux vivants* behind her house and with her failed attempt in 1904 to establish a writers' colony for women on Lesbos. In the Academy, Barney gathered around her, as had her model Sappho, the elite writers of her era, tried to create an atmosphere of sororal cooperation and support, and gave women writers a place to try out their unpublished works before their peers. In addition, Barney and the other wealthy members of the salon subsidized the printing of otherwise unpublishable works, much as Virginia Woolf and the Hogarth Press did in England. One of the major beneficiaries of the Academy was Djuna Barnes, whose *Ladies Almanack* was published thanks to donations and subscriptions undertaken in the Academy.[34] Barney also tried to establish a Renée Vivien literary award, as much to keep alive a name that was fast fading from public recognition as to support worthy writers. Unlike its French counterpart, the Academy did not exclude either sex, though most events seem to have been attended only by women. The Academy also subsidized several male writers, most notably Ezra Pound.

The Academy of Women was not comparable to contemporary women's salons, which, because of feminist consciousness about racism, classism, and other political considerations, admit all. As a result, the contemporary "salon," such as the defunct Women's Salon in New York, has been mostly an exercise in reading unpublished work to a packed throng, rather than an interchange among a select group of literary or artistic peers, followed by a delightful dinner, thoughtfully provided by the hostess. Although Barney considered herself a feminist, she was also an elitist, as she often admitted in her writings. No woman or man simply walked through her door: All came via an invitation or with invited guests. One had to prove that one *deserved* to be there. As Ned Rorem recounted to me, Natalie Barney told him that she was interested in a man only from the neck up, and demanded to know what he had to offer.[35]

Despite its political shortcomings, the salon was perhaps the only one of Barney's ideals that worked almost as well in practice as it did in fantasy. The salon met regularly until World War II and then resumed after the war had ended.

The elitist underpinnings of the salon should make the next era of Barney's life less difficult to comprehend, though my earlier account of Barney's transformation during World War II from pacifist to Fascist elicited great astonishment and bitter outcries of disappointment when it appeared.[36] Though we constantly witness vast transmutations in political stances—for instance, many often forget that Ronald Reagan began his political career as a liberal Democrat—feminist readers are thoroughly and rightfully disheartened when they learn of Barney's Fascist leanings. We wish to observe only the heroic tendencies of our feminist foremothers, but as Adrienne Rich has pointed out, to whitewash history in this fashion does none of us a service.

The roots of Barney's Fascism were always present. She fervently detested the masses. Naturally, the philosophy of Mussolini, who declared that one group was superior to another, coincided with Barney's own beliefs. Furthermore, she had decided some time before the war broke out never to return to the States, and Mussolini let Barney and others reside peacefully in Italy as long as they agreed with his politics. Barney needed little encouragement. In a journal she kept during World War II, she blamed the war on Churchill and the Jews, and quite contradicted the pride in being one-eighth Jewish that she had expressed at the turn of the century. Clearly, she had been proud of a slight trace of Jewish heritage so long as it was popular to claim that identity. When the label seemed dangerous, she discarded it like an old piece of clothing and even trotted out the old and vicious stereotypes of Jewish people. For instance, in a journal she kept during the war, she remarked that "the Jews first commercialized the world, then had a hand in running it."[37] She went so far as to encourage Ezra Pound to make his pro-Fascist broadcasts and gave him his first radio as a present.

In addition, Barney lacked a core of feminist support such as exists today. When she, along with a handful of her friends, opposed World War I, she was scoffed at by the majority of her friends, the "ambulance flies." A woman who valued friendship over politics, she was not apt to make an unpopular choice a second time. From where she sat in Paris and later in Florence, Fascism and anti-Semitism were definitely in vogue, and American Jews, such as Gertrude Stein and Alice B. Toklas, constituted such a tiny minority of her friends that they would have been unable to dissuade her from her beliefs, though there is no record that they tried.

After World War II, Barney was almost seventy years old and her political and literary activities were almost over, though she returned to Paris and reopened her salon, which met until her death. She published a few works, most of them, as I have stated, written previously, though she did collect and edit *In Memory of Dorothy Ierne Wilde,* as a celebration of her lover who had died during the war. She also wrote the introduction to *As Fine as Melanctha* by Gertrude Stein. Apparently, Barney's Fascist leanings did not end their friendship.

Barney's romantic escapades continued until the end of her life. In the 1950s, she met Janine Lahovary, with whom she initially had a secret affair because the latter was still married. By 1968, Brooks, who had waited over fifty years to have the ever-seductive Barney to herself, ended their relationship. The two never saw one another again. Brooks died in December 1970, Barney in February 1972.

Barney's life and beliefs—more so than Vivien's about whom too little is known—underscore the difficulties of writing a coherent feminist study of their works. Their lives and writings are fraught with what appear to be unbridgeable contradictions to contemporary feminists, who have a tendency to judge them by current feminist politics or literary theory. The dilemma is ours, really, not theirs. They did not view themselves as politically active feminists. They did not, for example, engage in the struggle for suffrage. Instead, they believed they lived on a poetic plane: Ultimately they followed the lyre of Sappho, not the temporary currents of politics.

And so we must judge their lives by the cloth of which they were made, neither covering up their abhorrent political ideologies nor forgetting the literary climate which gave birth to them. As we shall see, though they were in some ways much ahead of their times, in other ways, they were, like all of us, products of their era.

III.

GYNOCENTRICITY

Neither Natalie Barney nor Renée Vivien left behind a body of analytic or philosophic prose. As we have seen, Barney's characteristic mode was the epigram, that flash of wit which operates as an indicator of rational thought but which is ultimately incapable of logical development and which withers if subjected to rigorous analysis. Vivien was similarly disinterested in the systematic development of feminist theory; she preferred the allusiveness of Symbolist imagery in both her verse and her prose. Nevertheless, as a close analysis of the fictional works of both these writers indicates, their prose, like their poetry, arose out of deeply held and coherent convictions about the centrality of women and of women's values, the relative superiority of women, and the necessity to reclaim heroic female figures from their burial places in patriarchal history. Moreover, Renée Vivien was convinced that her primary audience was women, for whom she hoped to create new and more positive myths than those inherited from a masculinist past.

The choice of women as a specific, imagined audience is not as obvious as might at first appear. Most women writers were fully aware of the difficulties they faced in being taken seriously by the male literary establishment. Their struggle was for acceptance in the putatively genderless world of letters, a world which was, and which remains, heavily dominated by masculinist attitudes which were widely accepted as normative. Even so uncompromising a feminist as Virginia Woolf cautioned women writers in *A Room of One's Own* against closing themselves off in an aesthetic ghetto. Closer to the rue Jacob, Gertrude Stein's circle of aspiring and successful artists was almost exclusively male. The narrator in Stein's *Fernhurst* expresses this hostility and contempt for women as a class:

> I am for having women learn what they can but not to mistake learning for action nor to believe that a man's work is suited to them because they have

mastered a boy's education. In short I would have the few women who must do a piece of the man's work but think that the great mass of the world's women should content themselves with attaining to womanhood.[1]

Though Stein would certainly exempt herself and many of her friends from "the great mass of the world's women," the quotation reveals the difficulty that talented women have had in identifying themselves with the "ordinary" woman, a difficulty which Barney and, in a somewhat different way, Vivien shared. Barney, indeed, occasionally echoed the sentiment fashionable among intellectual women in the first half of this century that men were more interesting than women. She is quoted as having "suggested, long before her death, that her epitaph read: 'She was the friend of men and the lover of women, which, for people full of ardor and drive is better than the other way around.' "[2] Barney's wit here contradicts her fundamental feminism and is not characteristic of her most deeply held convictions. It is included precisely because it indicates the degree to which even Barney absorbed the prevailing inability to take women seriously.

It is in this context that Vivien's meditations on Sappho's poem about futurity seem the more significant. Sappho's speculation about her ultimate reputation does not specify the gender of her future admirers: "You may forget but / Let me tell you / this: someone in / some future time / will think of us."[3]

Vivien reworked these lines several times, each time making it clear that the audience for her own work would be female. This line appears in its finest version in "Vous pour qui j'écrivis" ("You for Whom I Wrote"): "You for whom I wrote, O beautiful young women! / You alone whom I loved, will you reread my verse . . . ? / Will you say, 'This woman had the ardor which eludes me . . . [sic] / Why is she not alive? She would have loved me. . . .' " [sic][4] This is a complex little fantasy in which Vivien not only imagines herself worthy of Sappho's love but, in turn, standing as a Sappho to generations of young women yet unborn, in a kind of unbroken line of female succession. She does not imagine a genderless or male future audience at last validating her work. Elsewhere, in a poem directly addressing her audience, "Voici ce que je chanterai" ("Here Is What I Will Sing"), Vivien announces: "Oh women! I sang in the hope of pleasing you."[5] One would have difficulty finding another woman poet of Vivien's generation, or indeed of any generation until the 1970s, who would admit to an imagined audience exclusively comprised of women; to do so would

seem to most women artists to be condemning themselves either to
triviality or marginality. In this regard, Vivien clearly anticipates the
commitment of much Lesbian/feminist poetry of the present moment.[6]

It was Vivien's passionate feminism which enabled her to commit
herself to an audience of women; that, and the sense which she shared
with Barney that women's creativity sprang more directly from unconscious sources than that of more logical, limited male artists. As Barney
remarked in *Thoughts of an Amazon,* "The Maenad, snatching the lyre of
Orpheus, / Submits the laws of Art to the laws of the Uterus."[7] Although
it is not clear what the "laws of the Uterus" may be, to suggest that
Orpheus, a favorite of the Symbolists of Barney's era, must step aside in
favor of the Maenad, whose creativity is centered in organs forever denied
the male, was both daring and provocative. This biological connection
provided the grounds for Vivien's mystical identification with women as a
kind of race, a correlation found in several of her poems. In "Les Succubes
disent . . ." ("The Succubuses Say . . ."), the poet announces: "We are no
longer of the race of men."[8] Throughout this poem, the *we* clearly refers
to "we women," especially women who are beyond the pale of respectability, such as the succubuses and banshees, specifically mentioned in this
poem. Vivien generalizes men, too, as a class: "Men will not see our
shadows on their doorsteps."[9]

Elsewhere, in "Union," Vivien again describes her intense identification with a female audience by using the word *nous* to embrace all
women:

Notre cœur est semblable en notre sein de
                                        femme,
Très chère! Notre corps est pareillement fait.
Un même destin lourd a pesé sur notre âme,
Nous nous aimons et nous sommes l'hymne
                                        parfait.

Je traduis ton sourire et l'ombre sur ta face.
Ma douceur est égale à ton grande douceur,
Parfois meme il nous semble être de même
                                        race . . .
J'aime en toi mon enfant, mon amie, et ma
                                        sœur.

Our hearts resemble each other's within our
                                        women's breast

So dear! Our body is similarly made.
The same heavy destiny has weighed on our
                                          souls,
We love each other, and we form a perfect hymn.

I can express your smile and the shadow on your
                                          face.
My gentleness equals your gentleness,
Sometimes it even seems that we belong to the
                                          same race . . .
In you I love my child, my friend, and my
                                          sister.[10]

In short, because of their shared anatomy, women have shared the same sad destiny. But, more positively, Vivien also expresses the conviction that women are sufficient unto themselves, for they can provide for each other all necessary connections: sister, mother, lover, friend, and child.

This sense of identification led Vivien in particular to re-examine the historical record for female figures with whom she could find communality. She paid as careful attention to those conventionally deemed evil as to the usual heroines, for she felt that these figures contained all women within themselves: "The mysterious breath of Lilith is in us."[11] In one of her most important poems, "Souveraines" ("Female Sovereigns"), Vivien celebrates the beauty, the challenges, and the triumphs of eleven historical and quasi-historical figures, including Lilith, Rhodopis, Bathsheba, Cleopatra, and Lady Jane Grey. An octave is devoted to each of these women's achievements, but the summation spoken by each woman is the same: "The fatal star of Beauty / I was not happy."[12] According to Vivien, no matter how beautiful the woman is and no matter what she has accomplished, the exceptional woman is always unhappy.

Vivien's poem celebrates not merely the famous but also the obscure: Campaspe, Pauline, Elizabeth Woodville, and Eleanor of Aquitaine; all are resurrected in something of the same spirit which animated Judy Chicago's *Dinner Party*. Natalie Barney was similarly interested in women's history—especially in what remained of the history of the matriarchies. The Amazons particularly attracted her, for they are mentioned in a number of her works, including *Adventures of the Mind* and *Traits and Portraits*, where she wonders how they lived and reproduced completely independently of men. In her unpublished autobiography, she states, "These legends seemed to me more interesting than the society to which I belonged."[13] What Remy de Gourmont may have intended as an amusing pun when he named her "L'Amazone" was to Barney, as it has been to later Lesbian/feminists like Monique Wittig, a sober and intriguing possibility.

In a certain sense, the historical researches of Barney and Vivien were animated by a somewhat different principle from that which caused them to deify Sappho, as we shall see in the next chapter. They found in Sappho what is at present termed a role model—an historical prototype which could serve as justification for their temerity in seizing for themselves, and for women in general, a centrally creative role. But whereas Sappho was by then secure in her position as a major poet, many of the female figures, such as Lilith and Vasthi, who interested Vivien in particular, were in rather ill repute. She saw her task as a rescue mission—to redeem these women from the condemnation called down on them by masculinist history in response to their actual virtues—rebelliousness, defiance, strength, and uncompromising purity. These characters receive their fullest development in Vivien's prose work, for Barney rarely took the trouble to treat them beyond a sketch in a sonnet or a few lines in her epigrams. Thus, it is mainly to Vivien that we must now turn for the working out of the redemption of feminist role models.

Two of the most significant exponents of female rebellion and defiance, Lilith and Vashti, are drawn from Biblical tradition. Their stories are similar since both record the fate of the defiant woman who is ultimately replaced by one more acquiescent to patriarchal demand. Lilith, created independently and equally to Adam, was banished when she refused to obey him. She was succeeded by Eve, made from Adam's rib. Vashti was the first wife of King Ahasuerus. When she refused to accede to his order to display herself unveiled before his court, she was exiled and replaced by Queen Esther. Although Esther is usually regarded as a heroine, Vivien clearly preferred Vashti. As Vivien's poetic counterpart, San Giovanni, remarks in *A Woman Appeared to Me:* "This Vashti . . . prouder and more beautiful than fearful Esther, once dazzled my imagination. . . ."[14] In Renée Vivien's treatment of Vashti in "Le Voile de Vasthi" ("The Veil of Vasthi") in *The Woman of the Wolf,* her disobedience is portrayed as a decidedly righteous act. King Ahasuerus is unquestionably wrong in demanding that Vashti unveil herself in front of his drunken courtiers. According to Vivien, the veil is not an oppressive imprisonment of women, but a voluntary protection of privacy against the impure glances of men, and Ahasuerus has no right to demand that Vashti display herself as one of his possessions. When she refuses to obey the king, her act is viewed not as the defiance of an obstinate wife, but as an act of revolution in the name of all women. Vashti tells the women in the harem and the seven eunuchs who have brought the king's order:

> "It was not just King Ahasuerus that I was thinking about when I acted. . . .
> For my action will reach all women, and they will say: 'King Ahasuerus
> had ordered Queen Vashti to be brought into his presence, and she did not
> go.' And from this day, the princesses of Persia and of Media will know that
> they are no longer the servants of their husbands, and that the man is no
> longer the master of his house, but that the woman is free and a mistress
> who is equal to the master in his house."[15]

Vashti's words of defiance, in which she calls attention to the political meaning of her act, strike a responsive chord of pride among the assembled noblewomen. Only a Jewish slave woman,[16] who has already told Vashti the story of Lilith as a warning against defiance, prophesies the suffering that follows rebellion, but Vashti is unmoved: "I would like to have been Lilith," she declares.[17] The king and the princes also understand the implications of Vashti's stand and, to prevent the spread of the rebellion to every household in the land, the king's counselors convince him to cast Vashti aside in favor of a new queen.

Vashti remains defiant; the women around her are horrified at the king's retribution. To Vashti, exile does not represent punishment but freedom—typically, for Vivien, the freedom of annihilation. Vashti does not wait to be stripped of her crown and jewels, symbols of her husband's power; rather, she removes them herself and dons the clothing of an old Jewish slave, now ripped in shreds as a sign of mourning. Then, with pride, and behaving as though her rags were a new court dress, she announces to the assembly that she will walk into the desert. The other women warn her that she will surely perish, but Vashti will not be dissuaded. She reminds the others of the universal significance of her act and again compares herself to Lilith: "Perhaps I will perish there [in the desert] of hunger. Perhaps I will perish there between the teeth of wild animals. Perhaps I will die there of loneliness. But, since the rebellion of Lilith, I am the first free woman."[18] With these words, she walks toward the desert and to her death. As is true of so many of Vivien's heroines, death and autonomy seem to be irrevocably linked. Vashti's choice strikes the reader as essentially positive and heroic, if unquestionably Romantic. The demand of Ahasuerus reveals to Vashti and to the assembled ladies that their apparent power is merely borrowed from the men who command them. When Vashti dons the rags of her slave, she indicates that their positions are interchangeable, that all women who accept life on the terms offered by men are, in fact, slaves. Yet, Vashti transforms these rags by her act and implies that some kind of liberation is theoretically possible. Under these circumstances, the only valid and authentic choice open to Vashti is the one she makes. It must also be pointed out that her fate is not absolutely sealed. "Perhaps I will perish there," but perhaps, on the other hand, she will survive, to live out her life in absolute freedom from the whims of kings.

Lilith, of course, is the prototype of Vashti's rejection of domination. She refused to obey Adam, and for that rebellion she was stricken from the Book of Life as a warning to all women. She survived in tradition as a kind of nightmare curse. According to Sandra Gilbert and Susan Gubar:

> . . . The figure of Lilith represents the price women have been told they must pay for attempting to define themselves. And it is a terrible price: cursed both because she is a character who "got away" and because she dared to usurp the essentially literary authority implied by the act of naming, Lilith is locked into a vengeance (child-killing) which can only bring her more suffering (the killing of her own children). And even the nature of her one-woman revolution emphasizes her helplessness and her isolation, for her protest takes the form of a refusal and a departure, a flight of escape rather than an active rebellion, like, say, Satan's.[19]

Vivien revived her as a heroine who preferred freedom to safety. According to Vivien, Lilith was allied to the Serpent, Vivien's symbol of female wisdom, rather than to Adam, who acted to protect male power. As Vivien describes her in "The Veil of Vashti": "She is like the supernatural dreams of hermits. She torments honest sleep with dreams. She is Fever, she is Desire, she is Perversity. In truth, Lilith has been punished for centuries because nothing will ever appease her hunger for the Absolute."[20]

Thus, Lilith is not merely the first failed woman. She is perhaps the conscience of mankind; she combines the madness of fever and desire with the perversity of the outcast. Her true crime is her hunger for the Absolute—that is, her quest for knowledge, her inability to compromise. It is likely, too, that Vivien sought to replace Orpheus with Lilith as a symbol of the quest for hermetic knowledge and also to enthrone her as the goddess of the truly decadent. She is perverse rather than pure; she inspires delirium more than salvation.[21]

The notion of Lilith as an epitome of female power is reiterated in the description of her which appears in the poem "Female Sovereigns": "I populated the universe with shades and demons. / Before Eve, I was the light of the world. / And I loved the perverse tempter, the Serpent. / I conceived the Unreal in my deep soul. / The Earth bowed before my royalty."[22] Lilith here appears as the supreme Earth Goddess. Whatever else she may represent, Vivien never portrays her as the traditional harpy, wailing in despair at her permanent exile from life. She appears instead as a provocative lost opportunity, a turn toward female power not taken, but not irrevocably lost.

Given the choice between compromise and death, Vivien's heroines unhesitatingly choose the latter. This characteristic is particularly present in the heroine of the title story of Vivien's collection, *The Woman of the Wolf.* The unnamed lady chooses to die in the embrace of her companion she-wolf rather than sacrifice the animal to obtain a place in a lifeboat.

As is the case with a number of other tales in this collection, the story is told from the point of view of a male narrator, one who reveals at least as much about himself in the course of his narration as he does about the subject of his story. This narrator is an ordinary bourgeois gentleman, a smug womanizer who offers the story of the lady as an after-dinner entertainment; he understands nothing of its meaning. The speaker, M. Lenoir, recounts the events on an ocean voyage on which he passed the time attempting to seduce the only woman passenger aboard ship, not because he was particularly smitten by her charms, but because there was no other woman around. He persistently misinterprets her unequivocal rejection of his advances as moves in an elaborate courtship game, for to do otherwise would injure his self-conceit. At last, he attributes her supreme lack of interest in him to her being Lesbian.

But he is as wrong here as in every other way. Although she far prefers women to men for their superior virtues of constancy, self-forgetfulness, patience, forgiveness, and chastity, the lady has never loved an individual woman: "I have observed women in passing who are noble in spirit and in heart. But I have never attached myself to them. Their gentleness even sets them at a distance from me. Since my spirit is not sufficiently lofty, I lose patience in the face of their excessive candor and devotion."[23]

She is attached only to her she-wolf, Helga, who is the visible symbol of her own inner essence—Helga is proud, aloof, self-contained, fierce, wild, intractable. It is this essence which forbids the lady's attachment to another woman, for she has never met one whose female gentleness has not led to a diminution of her freedom of spirit. The only fit consort for her chaste sexuality is her wolf, in whose embrace she dies.

The lady's wildness of spirit prevents her from loving a particular woman; her uncompromising candor and profound distaste for men make a heterosexual connection unthinkable. The lady may be an extraordinary woman, but as she responds to M. Lenoir's dishonest pursuit of a shipboard diversion with forthrightness and honesty, she shares every woman's frustration at ever being taken seriously in the world of men. Lenoir receives each of her heartfelt convictions with an amused condescension: His conceit requires him to attribute them to coquetry. At one point, she expresses her repugnance at the idea of a physical connection with a man: " 'Morally, he sickens me; physically, I find him repugnant. . . . I have seen men kissing women on the lips and obscenely pawing them. The spectacle of a gorilla would not be more repellant [sic].' "[24] In response to this strong statement, Lenoir merely reflects that she is here overplaying her role.

At the end of "The Woman of the Wolf," Lenoir's unbreachable conceit permits the reader to accept the lady's decision to drown as credible and even heroic. Lenoir represents the world of ordinary men; the lady's refusal to enter the lifeboat stands for her refusal to enter that world, to live closely with men to whom she is merely prey, to surrender her wild and virginal self, embodied in her wolf. To Lenoir, women have no existence except as the reflection of male ego; if the lady were to abandon her wolf-companion and enter the lifeboat, she would be confirming his view. Given the choice open to her, the lady's decision to drown is not, as Lenoir would have it, perverse or mad, but tragically inevitable and right.

But the lady is also heroic in a more ordinary sense. Like a number of other heroines in these stories, she excels at what are commonly considered male virtues. M. Lenoir admits to abject panic as the ship begins to sink. But the lady remains cool and unshaken. She is, indeed, the model of "masculine" virtue.

Much the same can be said of Nell in "Brune comme une noisette" ("The Nut-Brown Maid"). Not only is she calmly courageous like the lady, but she also takes the male prerogative of leadership: It is Nell who invites her companion, Jerry, for a deer hunt, she who picks the time and place, and she who borrows the dinghy from which they hope to hunt. Nell's hunting skills are considerably greater than those of Jerry; in fact, Nell can distinguish a deer from a bear by the way deer move their eyes: "Those are not the eyes of a deer. . . . [sic] They shine in a completely different manner; moreover, they are smaller and set farther apart. . . . The eyes of a deer don't move like that. Deer don't move their heads in irregular circles like that."[25]

Jerry is certainly no match for Nell's unique hunting techniques, and in any event, he seems much more interested in obtaining a kiss from the unwilling Nell than in procuring a hunting trophy for his wall. Thus, Nell must not only defend Jerry against his own incompetence as a woodsman, but she must also defend herself against his singularly ill-timed desires for a kiss. She has already rejected him once, saying, "I would prefer to swallow a toad than to let you kiss me,"[26] using the French expression for a particularly unacceptable task, but Jerry takes her literally, producing a toad which he challenges her to swallow or he will kiss her by force. Predictably, Nell downs the toad.

Jerry's petulance over his rejection and his inferior woodcraft make him seem "feminine" in comparison to the stoic Nell. The role reversal is emphasized in the final scene of the story. Jerry nearly brings disaster upon them by shooting a bear, which he mistook for a deer, without finishing off the beast. He begs Nell once more for a final kiss before their apparently inevitable death. She again refuses: " 'I can't, Jerry. Even before the great darkness, I can't . . . and nevertheless, I love you very much, my brother Jerry. . . .' "[27] For Jerry, this rejection is "more bitter than the idea of death,"[28] but for Nell, it is evidence of the utter seriousness of her commitment to physical inviolability, which, we may conclude, is the source of her strength. Jerry, on the other hand, is the romantic, seeking one last glamorous kiss before the final curtain is lowered.

Vivien was evidently fascinated with the possibilities inherent in the confrontation between men, women, and quintessential Nature, and she returned to the theme on several occasions. In the Romantic mode, Vivien often chooses settings that are exotic, improbable, or bizarre. It soon becomes apparent in "The Nut-Brown Maid" how little Vivien knows of certain periods of history or of life in the wild. This is clearly a "green world" fantasy, as documented in Annis Pratt's *Archetypal Patterns in Women's Fiction*. "The green world of the woman hero . . . [is] a place from which she sets forth and a memory to which she returns for renewal,"[29] but for Vivien the green world is not an aspect of devotion to nature as it is in many nineteenth-century English and American novels by women.

Vivien would probably argue that she hardly means for the reader to take her stories literally. As I stated in my introduction to *The Woman of the Wolf,* she "is not primarily concerned with the real world as we might recognize it. Her fantastic universe majestically floats several feet above the ground, never anchored firmly to reality by factual accuracy or believability."[30] Rather, Vivien is concerned with the psychological behavior of the sexes, which, she seems to imply, reverses itself quite dramatically from what would be considered "normative" when the forces of civilization are removed.

Vivien returned to this theme on several occasions, with varying degrees of success. Another story set in the North American wild is "La Soif ricane . . ." ("Snickering Thirst") in which two adventurers, Polly and Jim, make their way across the empty prairie. Vivien never bothers to explain the motives for this long, tiring journey.

It is the male character, Jim, who suffers from "female" weaknesses—particularly from a hyperactive imagination which prevents him from taking practical action when confronted by mortal danger. Paralyzed by terror, he faints when threatened with immediate death in a prairie fire. The phlegmatic Polly saves both their lives with a stratagem straight out of James Fenimore Cooper's *The Prairie:* She sets a counterblaze which the prairie fire cannot cross. (Why they are not incinerated on the spot remains unclear both to the reader, and one suspects, to Vivien; again, practical woodcraft was not her strong suit. Like Cooper's original prairie, this is a literary wilderness.)

Polly's sangfroid contrasts vividly with Jim's cowardly behavior. Further, the fact that she is stronger and cleverer than Jim and can drink more than he does not endear her to Jim nor inspire him with gratitude for saving his life. On the contrary, he vows to kill her at the earliest opportunity in revenge for her revealing his cowardice to himself.

Beyond these simple role reversals, Vivien is concerned with working out the consequences of the appearance of a liberated life for all women in a world of men whose primary motivation is the protection of their own egos. The challenge presented by the independent woman, such as Polly, frequently occasions murderous impulses in the male who experiences female autonomy as a mortal threat. Luckily, in some cases, the male character is so comparatively weak that he can only swear a silent revenge on the woman who is unselfconsciously braver than he is. Jim, in "Snickering Thirst," is such a character, but though his threats may be futile against the healthy Polly, we are not convinced that he has always been so harmless. In the course of his nightmarish trek across the prairies, he is obsessed with a recurrent memory of a mysterious pale woman, who appears to represent his ideal of what a proper woman ought to be. Repelled by Polly's ruddy cheeks, he remembers ". . . a pale, thin face [he] . . . had once loved. . . . [He] . . . adored the shadow of her eyelashes on her pale cheeks."[31] But what became of this paragon of feminine charm? Jim cannot remember: "I don't even know anymore if that odd little girl who read for those long hours is living or dead. I believe she must be dead because sometimes I feel such an emptiness in my heart!" After a pause, he adds, "But I am not sure of anything."[32]

Significantly, he is also unclear about why he took up his present unlikely occupation as "prairie rider." The reader is left to speculate that perhaps the death of the pale woman and Jim's flight to the oblivion of the wasteland are in some way related.

The connection Vivien makes between male sexuality and murder is overtly stated in several stories in this collection. It is in "La Saurienne" ("The Crocodile Lady"), however, that Vivien most clearly reveals what she believes to be the sources of this deadly confusion between lust and homicide. "The Crocodile Lady" is yet another green world story, this one set apparently in Africa. The narrator, Mike Watts, remembers a hallucinatory journey across the desert, in the course of which he encounters a woman, the Crocodile Lady, who bears a striking resemblance to a reptile. As in other tales of this genre, "the hero not only appreciates and likes nature but, through a process of metamorphosis, *becomes* an element in it."[33] The Crocodile Lady is evidently intended to be taken as some sort of lesser earth-goddess or " 'lady of the beasts,' "[34] one who has friends in high places:

> "The king and the queen of the crocodiles are my intimate friends," she continued. "The king lives at Denderah. The queen, who is as powerful as he and even more cruel, preferred to go forty leagues higher up the river, in order to reign by herself. She wants undivided power. He loves his independence also; as a result, they live separately, while remaining very good friends. They meet only occasionally, in order to make love."[35]

In the natural world of which the Crocodile Lady is an emissary, female and male wield equal, if separate, power. In a grotesque act of seduction, the Crocodile Lady demonstrates her closeness to the power of Nature by plunging into the river and riding the back of a crocodile. When she emerges unscathed from this act of daring, she evidently expects Mike Watts to be overcome with admiration and to fall into her arms. He is, instead, overcome with terror. It is difficult to say which frightens him more—the Crocodile Lady's evident power or her sexual aggressiveness. In any event, he saves himself from what he sees as a fate worse than death by killing her in a particularly revolting and brutal way—he gouges out her eyes, the only part of her body that is vulnerable to his knife.

In recounting his deed, Watts takes great pains to underscore its significance to him: "I carved out her eyes, I tell you. Oh, one thing I am is courageous, for sure! You can say all sorts of malicious things about me, but you can never make out that I am a coward. Lots of men in my predicament would have lost their heads. But me, I didn't hesitate for a second. . . ."[36] In fact, Mike lost his head from the moment he saw the Crocodile Lady. That spectacle of absolute female power totally petrified him; his only thought was to destroy it. In his eyes, the Crocodile Lady is physically hideously repellent. Also, as Annis Pratt points out, "the fact that freely undertaken sexual choices of any kind contradict patriarchal expectations for women accounts for the scorn heaped upon women . . . ,"[37] such as the Crocodile Lady. Furthermore, he is oblivious to her uniqueness, her mystery. Above all other considerations, Watts needs to demonstrate that his male identity has emerged intact from this encounter; he is no coward.

In this story, Vivien totally reverses not merely the usual sexual roles, but also a typical motif of her own stories, perhaps in order to reflect upon the differences she perceives between male and female natures. Mike Watts is about to be raped; like the typical Vivien heroine, he chooses death rather than dishonor. But because he is a man, he does not choose his own death—he chooses to kill. The ideal Vivien heroine, faced with the violation of her chastity or her autonomy, usually exercises her freedom by selecting the moment of her own death with dignity. The male destroys.

This is a motif repeated in a posthumously published work, *Anne Boleyn*, in which the tragic second wife of Henry VIII is interpreted as a martyr to patriarchal pride. Vivien's attention was drawn to her subject by two biographies written toward the turn of the century by Mary Strickland and W. H. Dixon. Although both of these were written in English, curiously Vivien asked Charles-Brun and Willy to translate them for her into French as she was apparently and inexplicably no longer able to read her native tongue.[38]

Perhaps because of her own increasing interest in Catholicism, in this work Vivien seems to be attempting to find in modern history a counterpart to her earlier, pre-Christian heroines, Vashti and Lilith. A repeated description of Anne Boleyn characterizes her as "this woman, who was a worker for the Reformation, died Catholic,"[39] an ironic contradiction which is reminiscent of Vivien herself: Born Protestant, she became a self-described pagan and may have died a Catholic.

The religious theme is underscored by the structure of this novel, a fact overlooked by Jean-Paul Goujon, who rediscovered the printer's proofs of *Anne Boleyn* and who wrote the introduction for it. The novel consists of forty-two extremely short chapters, considering that the novel is only one hundred and two pages long. Some chapters consist of only one sentence, or perhaps a few lines. Transition is replaced by the repetition of important lines or ideas from preceding chapters. The redundancy lends an intense, almost dogmatic flavor to the work, and one is left with the impression of a clear intent on Vivien's part to imitate the style of parts of the Bible. Through this association, the drama of Anne Boleyn is elevated to an even higher plane than that of mere fiction.

The themes, however, closely follow those of Vivien's other works. Like the heroines of "Female Sovereigns," Anne Boleyn "bore the sorrow of her beauty and of her intelligence, for which she died more horribly."[40] But Vivien was attracted as much by Boleyn's defiance of Henry's desires as she was by the pathos of her death. Boleyn, mother of Elizabeth (and thus of the great Virgin Queen), adamantly refuses to try a third pregnancy after the death of her first son: *"You will get no more boy's [sic] by me."*[41] In Vivien's view, it is this defiance that leads to Boleyn's death. Popularly, Anne Boleyn is viewed as a passive victim of Henry's lust and ambition. Characteristically, Vivien endows her with will: Her freedom consists in the act of choosing death. As was true of Vashti, Lilith, and the Woman of the Wolf, death is far less menacing than the prospect of a life of submission.

Henry, like some of Vivien's other male characters (Mike Watts, for example), easily juxtaposes lust and homicide. Henry courts Anne before he has divorced his first wife, Catherine. When Anne defies Henry by not giving him what he most desires, a son, his lust quickly turns to murderous rage. Yet, for all his temporal power, Vivien depicts Henry as a coward. "Henry VIII, who had never been brave, became frightened."[42] And most condemning of all in Vivien's eyes, "Henry VIII feared death."[43]

Yet although the reader may admire the steadfastness and courage which permit Vivien's heroines uncompromisingly to die rather than surrender, they seem excessively eager to seize the opportunity. Frequently, they seem less to be bowing to sad necessity than to be joyously embracing oblivion as a kind of ultimate sexual thrill. Andromeda, chained to her rock in "Blanche comme l'écume" ("White as Foam"), gazes out to sea, awaiting the advent of the monster who will devour her: "A sob of terror and love burst from Andromeda's lips. Her eyelids fluttered before they closed before the exquisite delight expressed in his face. On her lips was the bitter taste of Death."[44]

Perseus, therefore, receives a less than enthusiastic welcome:

"Why could you not let me perish in the grandeur of Sacrifice? The beauty of my incomparable Destiny intoxicated me and now you have ravished me with a Lethean kiss. O Perseus, understand that only the Sea Monster has known my sob of desire, and that Death seemed to me less oppressive than your impending, suffocating embrace."[45]

The price of Andromeda's salvation, we recall, was her marriage to Perseus, a condition about which she was never consulted. To this extent, she conforms with the favorite Vivien heroine who prefers death to coercion. But Andromeda anticipates death with pleasure; before Perseus even appears, we discover that "not in the least did she fear chaste-eyed Death, solemn-handed Death; what she feared was Love, ravager of spirit and flesh."[46] At this point, we suspect that Vivien's heroines defend their virginity less as a way of maintaining their autonomy than out of repugnance at the demands their own bodies are likely to make on their idealized visions of themselves.

A similar celebration of virginity may be found in Vivien's novel *A Woman Appeared to Me*. Although Vally flirts with men from time to time, the narrator finds this rather low and disgusting. When Dagmar marries, the narrator is completely distraught:

The day of her marriage, I was saddened over this virginal grace about to be barbarously immolated. Hideous maternity would deform her sexless body. And conjugal rutting would defile her flesh, once pure like tender eglantines. . . .

I remained inconsolable in the face of the deflowering of a dream. . . .[47]

Vivien's narrator's distress arises from the destruction of a "dream" of the ideal self as much as it does from her disgust at heterosexual connection and the processes of reproduction. Elsewhere in the novel, the narrator characterizes the act of taking a woman's virginity as follows: " '*Let the act of sexual initiation be as cowardly as pillage, as brutal as plunder, as bloody as a massacre, and worthy only of drunken and barbarous army rabble.*' "[48] Here the taking of a woman's virginity is viewed as an act of war. Thus, men who assault women's chastity are seen in this passage as the soldiers of men's war against women. It is a war which has only one goal:

"Now, the only goal of the actions of men has always been to subjugate women to their stupid caprices, to their sensuality, and their unjust and ferocious tyranny. And how can you not hate an individual who presents himself to you as your master? Any intelligent and proud being will necessarily revolt against the yoke of another being, who is sometimes his equal, but most often, his inferior."[49]

Although these long speeches, the first by San Giovanni and the second by the narrator's beloved Vally (Barney's counterpart in the novel), are interjected into the novel with somewhat of a soapbox fervor, they show that as a group Vivien's heroines transcend the overfastidious neurotics that individually they may be charged with being. In the world as Vivien saw it, the strong or exceptional woman—the Woman of the Wolf, Polly, Nell, the Crocodile Lady—will arouse in the ordinary male a mixture of lust and murderousness. "As in novels characterized by the green-world archetypes, we see men pictured as agents of harsh disruption. . . ."[50] Outside the world of nature, the beautiful and pure woman, such as Anne Boleyn or Vashti, will likewise stimulate lust and the desire to dominate. In either case, the combined strength of males acting in concert to protect each other is too great for such women to hope to overcome by themselves, and Vivien's imagination did not extend to the prospect of women acting collectively in their own defense. Therefore, given the very limited possibilities of these circumstances, the only honorable course for the heroine to take was to choose the moment and the manner of her death with dignity.

If Vivien saw any hope for survival without compromise, it was in the possibility of establishing a pocket of separate existence, as far as possible from the threat of male control. In a poem "Nous irons vers les poètes" (We Will Go towards the Poets"), she describes this idealized state:

> Les blâmes des humains ont pesé sur nos
> > fronts,
> Mais nous irons plus loin. Là-bas, nous
> > oublierons . . .
> Sous un ciel plus clément, plus doux, nous
> > oublierons . . .
>
> Nous souvenant qu'il est de plus larges
> > planètes,
> Nous entrerons dans le royaume des poètes,
> Ce merveilleux royaume où chantent les poètes.
>
> La lumière s'y meut sur un rythme divin.
> On n'a point de soucis et l'on est libre enfin.
> On s'étonne de vivre et d'être heureux enfin.

The blame of humans has weighed on our heads,
But we will go far away. Over there, we will
                                          forget . . .
Under a more clement and gentler heaven, we
                                will forget . . .

We will remember that there are bigger planets.
We will enter into the kingdom of the poets,
This marvellous kingdom where the poets sing.

There the light fades with a divine rhythm.
They have no worries and they are free at last.
They are astonished to be alive and happy at
                                          last.[51]

The word *we* for Vivien always implies women, and this new world of beauty and freedom to which they might go, if it could exist at all in the physical universe, would be open to the few, the talented, and the wealthy. It was not a world to replace the present order, but one which offered an escape from it for those who could afford, and who deserved, to go. It was this world that Vivien hoped to establish on Lesbos with Natalie Barney, but as they discovered to their dismay, even that shrine to Sappho had been corrupted beyond redemption by the heavy hand of man.

There is ample evidence in the work of Barney that she was in substantial theoretical agreement with Vivien's views on the oppressive nature of men and on the natural antagonism between men and women. For example, an entire section of Barney's *Thoughts of an Amazon* is entitled "The War between the Sexes."[52] The difference between them seems more one of temperament than of ideology. Vivien was the far more serious writer of the two. Barney was content to jot down her "scatterings" and to leave them to the reader—and perhaps to Vivien—to flesh out. Barney was apparently disinterested in persuading the audience of her point of view by creating literary models; she believed her wit alone would suffice. It is a sad irony that Barney, who lived to be ninety-five, wrote only one novel and did not produce a single extant short story whereas Vivien, in her short lifespan of thirty-two years, penned two volumes of short stories and two novels. Further, while Barney wrote over ten plays, including one she co-authored with her mother, Alice Pike Barney, she did not rewrite, polish, or improve any of her plays to the point where they could be professionally mounted. She contented herself with amateur productions in her own garden near the Temple of Friendship.

Since Barney's strongest talent was her creation of *bons mots*, it was logical for her to turn to writing plays in which the characters could give utterance to her witty epigrams. Indeed, some of Barney's cleverer "scatterings" do appear in almost identical form in her plays.[53] Yet, even Shakespeare did not construct a play merely on the basis of his scintillating lines, for any drama must have a comprehensible plot, a logical setting, and believable characters. Barney had little talent for constructing these last three components; her plays, most of which lie gathering dust at the Bibliothèque Doucet, would probably baffle even the most sympathetic audience. Therefore, it is not possible to analyze the plot and the characters, including their motivations, to the extent that one can examine the works of Vivien. The plays and her epigrams, however, do reveal some interesting concepts, which can be examined for the views they express about the nature of men and women, about which Barney seemed to be in substantial agreement with Vivien.

Again, the difference between Vivien and Barney seems more one of temperament than of ideology: Vivien, as we have seen, experienced a profound revulsion from men—their physical nature repelled her. Barney, on the other hand, was less troubled by men's physical existence—she had a positive preference for women but was willing to grant to men a common humanity. Therefore, male characters, when they appear in Barney's work, are treated with a greater degree of sympathy than they receive in Vivien's short stories. (Male characters do not appear at all in Vivien's plays.) Nevertheless, Barney appeared to agree with Vivien's analysis of the source of women's oppression. In one of her published plays, "Autour d'une victoire" ("Around a Victory"), Barney portrayed men as women's masters, as perpetrators of crimes against women and children. The antagonist of the play, Démétrios, has conquered not only Athens but also the heart of Deïs, a virgin sculptress with whom all the men of the city are in love. When Deïs realizes that Démétrios is more interested in his conquest of her, which he perceives as an extension of his conquest of Athens, than he is in her love, she bitterly rejects him and enumerates his crimes:

> . . . vos victimes
> Des femmes, des enfants—des lâchetés, vos
> crimes!
> Et c'est vous, cœurs vénals, vous qui nous
> repoussez
> Vous, nos maîtres hautains, vous qui vous
> émpoussez

Dans l'orgie, et repus, vos vertus pantelantes.
Voulez juger! savoir, vos mains encore
                                              sanglantes
De quelque guerre obscure aux vils entassements
Si on est digne ou non de vos embrassements!
La plus basse hétaire est digne, et plus que
                                              digne
De vous. . . .

. . . your victims
Women, children—cowardices, your crimes!
And it's you, men of venal hearts, you who
                                              disgust us
You, our haughty masters, you who sink
                                              yourselves
Into orgies, and disgusted, your virtues
                                              twitching,
You wish to judge! To know! Your hands still
                                              bloody
From some obscure war with vile heaps of bodies
Whether they are worthy or not of your
                                              affections
The lowest courtesan is worthy, more than
                                              worthy
Of you. . . .[54]

Thus, despite a greater toleration of individual men, Barney's anger at men as a class is fully comparable with Vivien's. At this passage indicates, Barney agreed with Vivien that the lowest of women is superior to the best of men. In the section of her *pensées* devoted to the antagonism between the sexes, Barney once joked: " '. . . And on the last day, God created man.' We resent the fatigue of the Creator."[55] In the same volume, Barney put forth the notion that the female has a superior intelligence to that of the male: "A stupid woman is an anomaly, a contradiction. Women are foolish only inasmuch as they are not women."[56]

Barney also believed, with Vivien, that women are the victims of men's carnal aggressiveness, as we see in "Around a Victory" and in one of Barney's unpublished plays, "Le Mystère de Psyché" ("The Mystery of Psyche"). In the beginning of the latter play, Eros and Aphrodite debate the nature of men and women. Aphrodite takes a dim view of the lot of her mortal counterparts: "Raped, impregnated, abandoned . . . : These three acts form the entire life of a woman."[57] The second act becomes a practical demonstration of the differences between men and women, as Eros and Aphrodite compete for the love of the same woman, Psyche, who is inexplicably the beauty queen of 1933. Eros' carnal aggressiveness is rejected in favor of Aphrodite's gentle charm, though Psyche is unaware at this point that Aphrodite is a woman. Aphrodite makes a better suitor because she has all the grace of a woman and none of the lust both Barney and Vivien associated with men.

Barney claimed in her epigrams that her opinion of men arose not from ignorance, but from too great an acquaintance: "It is not because I don't think about men that I don't like them, but because I *do* think about them."[58] She had no doubt about the root cause of human conflict: "There is no sexual enemy: The enemy of man is man."[59]

Although Vivien competently describes the unwitting self-revelation of her male characters, they all reveal the same nature: They are the murderous antagonists of women. Only their monumental conceit and the cooperation of other men identical to themselves prevent them from recognizing their monstrous natures. Barney was willing to grant to men a greater variety of motivations and a larger range of character traits, despite the limited development of her plays. Thus, Barney's male characters are less projections emanating from a cosmic war against women than they are ordinary character-types possessed of common weaknesses.

Barney's sensibility is best portrayed in one of her unpublished plays, "Her Legitimate Lover." The plot is clearly borrowed from Oscar Wilde's *The Importance of Being Earnest*, in that the protagonists of both plays wish to avoid responsibility for their behavior. Horace, in Barney's play, is an energetic philanderer, pursuing all the women in the play—Penelope, Hope, Mrs. Muck, and the Duchess of Oldmeadow. All the while, he is married to May, Lady Downham. While Vivien would have transformed Horace into a lustful destroyer of women's virtue, Barney gives Horace a rudimentary sense of honor which prevents him from appearing as an unmitigated villain. In fact, the farce ends happily in a blissful reunion of May and Horace while Penelope is reunited with her former fiancé, Algy.

Perhaps because Barney granted men less power than did Vivien, she was capable, on occasion, of blaming women for their own difficulties, in a way not uncommon among exceptional women who have been unusually successful. She once complained in her *Thoughts of an Amazon* that "if women do not yet know how to be free—whether they are wives, courtesans, lovers, or slaves—it is only a question of class, temperament, chance . . . or weariness."[60] Even so, the list of situations of bondage for women is telling, and acerb.

One might expect, given their generally negative view of the prospect for fruitful relations between the sexes, that both Barney and Vivien would have developed an ideal heroine characterized primarily by strength of purpose and resoluteness of conviction rather than by physical beauty. Certainly, as we have seen, Vivien does indeed invent such figures, especially in her wilderness fiction, and Barney alludes to an Amazonian potential in her autobiography and in several places in her epigrams. But as often as not, the strong heroine in a Vivien short story is not particularly beautiful, and the one who in some ways is the strongest of all, the Crocodile Lady, is distinctly ugly. Ironically, their Symbolist inheritance led both Barney and Vivien to erect an ideal of beauty which was inevitably embodied in a female figure who was inactive, motionless, and pale. Curiously, in much of her poetry, Vivien yearns after a woman who bears a striking resemblance to the pale, dead woman who troubles the mind of the narrator in "Snickering Thirst." The women she apostrophizes look nothing whatever like the hearty heroine of that story or like the Crocodile Lady.

In part, this seeming contradiction is explained by the fact that both writers wanted women to be as little like men as possible. In their view, it was the soft, nurturing, emotional side of women that truly distinguished them from men. Liane de Pougy, in discussing her relationship with Barney, tried to explain in a journal entry the feminine values that women sought in other women at that time: "We loved long hair, pretty breasts, pouts, simpering airs, charm, grace; we didn't like women-boys very much. 'Why would anyone wish to resemble her enemies?' murmured Natalie-Flossie [Barney] in her little nasal voice."[61] Clearly, Barney and her contemporaries sought women, not "imitation men." There is an indication here of intense philosophical and sexual woman-centeredness; it was important for women to retain their essential and outward femininity, characteristics which they evidently believed were innate, not socially produced. Therefore, Vivien did not have to explain, even to herself, why she was able to praise the conventionally feminine virtue of fragility in her poetry. In "Je t'aime d'être faible . . ." ("I Love You for Being Weak"), the unidentified narrator addresses an unidentified woman in a poem which is indeed a litany of the charms of frailty:

> Je t'aime d'être faible et câline en mes bras
> Et de chercher le sûr refuge de mes bras
> Ainsi qu'un berceau tiède où tu reposeras. . . .

> Je t'aime d'être lente et de marcher sans bruit
> Et de parler très bas et de haïr le bruit,
> Comme l'on fait dans la présence de la nuit.

I love you for being weak and tender in my arms
And for looking for the safe refuge of my arms
Like a warm cradle where you will rest. . . .

I love you for being slow and for walking
                                        without noise
And for speaking very low and for hating noise.
As one behaves in the presence of night.[62]

The image of the frail beauty so ephemeral that her footsteps make no noise may seem almost comical to modern-day feminists, but her image haunts the poems of Renée Vivien. It might be an image of the Virgin so pure that her passing makes no impression on the universe except as an idea. In a world where action itself is potentially corrupting, this distilled essence of female beauty may serve a recuperative function. As Vivien noted in "Mains sur un front de malade" ("Hands on the Forehead of a Sick Woman"), posthumously published in 1910:

Les douces mains de femme ont des gestes de
                                        prêtre
Et répandent en vous la paix et le bien-être,
La consolation que vient donner le prêtre!

Elles n'apprennent point le geste qui guérit,
Elles l'ont toujours su . . . Dans l'horreur de la
                                        nuit
Cette imposition très calme nous guérit . . .

The gentle hands of a woman have the touch of
                                        a priest
And spread peace and well-being in you,
The consolation that the priest comes to give!

They don't have to learn the touch which cures.
They have always known it . . . In the horror of
                                        night
This calm laying on of hands cures us . . .[63]

Vivien makes it clear that women do not choose to enter this priesthood of beauty and consolation; it is their natural calling.

Closely connected with this worship of an ideal beauty was Vivien's celebration of a kind of pagan nudity. In an article on Renée Vivien, Jean Venettis clearly saw this connection: "It is through her love of artistic nudity (this sport which was exercised in antiquity) and through her cult of beauty . . . that Renée Vivien is a pagan. She goes beyond all the pales and all the prejudices of any theological particularism."[64] What Venettis fails to note is how this pagan conception of beauty may have been influenced by the work of Leconte de Lisle, especially his poem, *Hypathie*. "In *Hypathie* we find a complete expression of the poet's chief ideal, the ideal of beauty. . . . In contrast with Christianity we find the religious and philosophical thought of Greece, with its veneration for beauty—the quintessence of all that is human."[65] How easy Renée Vivien would have found it to identify with Hypathia, who revived the teachings of Plato in Alexandria only to be killed by the Christian mobs.[66] Like Leconte de Lisle, Vivien's worship of the naked body was not merely part of an attempt to return to a pre-Christian liberation from physical and psychological restraint, as it may have been for others of their contemporaries who similarly praised the virtues of nudity. In some ways, making the unclothed female body a positive value was a symbolic gesture repudiating the misogyny of the world around them, which found in the naked female a source of shame. For Vivien and Leconte de Lisle, nudity was a part of beauty, the worship of which has survived Christianity. The poet still sings, according to Lisle, "The melodious hymn of Holy Beauty!"[67] Ironically, as we shall see, there is always an element of chastity for Vivien, even in her most intense meditations on the female form in all its beauty.

For Barney, as it had been for Christine de Pisan, the female body was a country under attack by misogynist males. When Gomez de la Serna published an essay attacking breasts, Barney took up the challenge and responded in an essay which defended breasts and, by implication, the perfection of the female body: "In defending breasts against your errors and your masculine incomprehensions, I feel as if I am to some degree defending my country!"[68] De la Serna offered his attack on the female breast under the guise of an aesthetic preference; Barney recognized it for what, in fact, it was—a political attack on a female way of being and seeing.

Barney, particularly in her early poetry, lavishly praised female beauty. Like Vivien, she could perceive this beauty with a double vision—that is, worshipping both the abstract and the concrete simultaneously, as she does in her first volume of poems: "Flower among flowers, beauty among beauties, / I would like to sing you a sonnet of stars, / And chastely cover my words with veils. . . ."[69] Barney's pragmatic tastes, however, generally obscured her artistic quest for beauty, and she preferred to quip: "My only books / Were women's looks."[70]

As we shall see, the contradiction between the frail, ephemeral beauty and the hearty but typically plain heroine was not the only contradiction in the writings of Barney and Vivien. However, despite their failure to develop a cohesive and unified philosophy, their gynocentric stories and poems charted new territory for women as writers and readers. As Joanna Russ has noted, "An examination of English literature, or Western literature (or Eastern literature, for that matter) reveals that of all the possible actions people can do in fiction, very few can be done by women."[71] She later concludes, "Our literary myths are for heroes, not heroines. . . ."[72] The only role left for the woman is as "the protagonist of a Love Story."[73] This categorization of women in literature had been true from Eve to Emma Bovary. What Barney and especially Vivien in her tales tried to do was to create new options for female characters. As simplistic as they sometimes seem, their stories recycle the stuff of myths from the Bible to tales of the jungle and move women to the center stage as heroines, not as ingenues, virtuous mothers, vamps, camp followers, saints, martyrs, or other types usually left to single women. Vivien in particular transformed the passive heroine—waiting to be rescued from the villain, from nature, or from her own weaknesses—into the female hero, a woman who makes decisions and who acts, even if action usually leads to untimely death or inevitable destruction. She reclaimed the disparaged woman, such as Lilith and Vashti, and gave her back her dignity.

That they reconstituted familiar stories was a clever tactic, for "something that has been worked on by others in the same culture, something that is 'in the air' provides a writer with material that has been distilled, dramatized, stylized, and above all, clarified. A developed myth has its own form, its own structure, its own expectations and values, its own cues-to-nudge-the-reader."[74] As Russ points out, no one has ever faulted Milton, Shaw, Joyce, or Dickens, to name but a few, for borrowing from other sources.[75] By starting with a familiar tale—whether it is Vashti in a harem out of the *Arabian Nights* or Nell crossing the prairies in a parody of Cooper—Vivien cushions the reader by giving her a soothing frame of reference before the entire cultural terminology is turned on its head. What begins as a familiar tale of a hunt of a prairie fire ends as a lesson in women's courage and endurance, of women's self-determination, even in the face of death.

"At the heart of these transformations lies a startlingly radical core of perception about the profound antagonism between the psyches of men and women and about the potentialities of women sprung loose from conventional stereotypical behavior."[76] Both Barney and Vivien also explored the war between the sexes in an unapologetic way that suggested that all men "are locked in a self-protective impregnable egotism, which assumes a kind of gender solidarity from other men and which demands passive support from all women. When this support is withheld, or worse, when this smug self-satisfaction is challenged by women who refuse to accede to their demands, the men turn killer."[77]

On the other hand, neither Barney nor Vivien ever pretended to, or aspired toward, the leadership of a mass movement of women, a development toward which they were both supremely indifferent. In this regard, they were far less political than Virginia Woolf, who, in *A Room of One's Own* and *Three Guineas,* at least addressed the concerns of large numbers of women who might perhaps form such a movement.

Nevertheless, it must be said in their defense that both Barney and Vivien were determined that inherited myth and symbol could be transformed to work for, rather than against, women. Despite some flaws of style and characterization, both writers exhibited provocative daring in proffering visions of female heroism so contradictory to those of their predecessors and contemporaries. Both Barney and Vivien must have hoped that like the followers of Vashti, their readers would draw the proper conclusion from the rebellion of their heroines and the behavior of their male antagonists and find that a different world was in order, one where different options would be open to all.

IV.

SAPPHO AND OTHER GODDESSES

Women who, like Barney and Vivien, consciously sought to re-establish a primary role for female sensibility in the late nineteenth century faced a certain difficulty. Historically, the number of women who could claim the first rank as poets was very small. Although women had always been warmly welcomed in the French tradition as handmaidens to the arts or as muses, their potentiality as primary creators was viewed as dubious, at best. Thus it was a happy accident of history that the discovery of five new Sapphic fragments in Egypt in 1897[1] generated renewed interest in Sappho at about the same time that Barney and Vivien were beginning to write in Paris.

On all counts, Sappho was an appropriate choice to be the model and inspiration for Barney and Vivien, for she was the sole person about whom they were in absolute agreement. Her work, or what was left of it, had been revered since the Renaissance in France; it had influenced an impressive series of male poets; and, since so little firm knowledge existed of either Sappho's life or of much of her work, she could be, and had been, recreated in the image of her followers, who found in her, or imputed to her, those characteristics they felt most deeply expressed themselves. For the male followers of Sappho, she was an example of a fine and passionate lyricism. To Barney and Vivien, she was that and much more: She was a woman who had spent her life passionately involved with other women, had written about that passion, and had succeeded in establishing a school of women poets, a fact which confirmed their profound conviction that artistic creativity was not aberrant in women. Thus they formed an intense psychic bond with Sappho and examined her work minutely for any suggestion upon which they could erect a modern Sapphism. As Susan Gubar notes, "Precisely because so many of her original Greek texts were destroyed, the modern woman poet could write 'for' or 'as' Sappho and thereby invent a classical inheritance of her own."[2]

The ascertainable facts about Sappho's life were very few, but they were encrusted with a palimpsest of legend which was immensely provocative. She was born during an age and in a place where women were demonstrably able to pursue an intellectual and creative life in a way they never would again in later Classical history. She may or may not have married; she may or may not have been the mother of a daughter, Cleïs; she was evidently forced into exile for a period away from her beloved Lesbos; she may or may not have loved the famous ferryman, Phaon, and, despairing of his love, she may or may not have leaped from the Leucadian cliff. She definitely was the center of a school of younger women poets to some of whom she might have addressed passionate love lyrics, of which only fragments remain.[3]

Post-Classical considerations of Sappho have tended to center on her sexuality. For the most part, later interpretations of the Sapphic myth have concentrated on the heterosexual possibilities, and there are any number of versions in French, English, and German of the famous Leucadian Leap. Yet there remained a stubborn core of those whose interest was more taken by the homosexual implications of Sappho's verse than by the apparent heterosexual conversion suggested by her passion for Phaon. Among these were Baudelaire and Swinburne, but the most important predecessor for Barney and Vivien was Pierre Louÿs, whom they both knew. In 1899 or 1900, Barney read *The Songs of Bilitis*,[4] which had been published in 1894. *The Songs of Bilitis* was an extraordinary literary hoax in which Louÿs masqueraded as a contemporary of Sappho to produce a volume of erotic prose poems, complete with invented bibliography and textual notes. Barney greatly admired the book and showed it to Renée Vivien, who shared her admiration for it.

Although *The Songs of Bilitis* was not, as it purported to be, a translation of an ancient Greek text, it was solidly grounded in Louÿs' own Classical scholarship, and it suggested some exciting possibilities. To the aesthetes of the turn of the century, Classical Greece appeared as a liberating alternative to the petit-bourgeois values of the present age. Works such as *Bilitis* suggested that Greek culture could be brought forward and recreated in the modern world. For example, in the second section of *Bilitis*, Louÿs develops Mnasidika, a follower of Sappho, into a complete personality. "Elégies à Mytilène" ("Elegies to Mytilene") is itself a total reconstruction of life on Mytilene and is founded on the few remaining fragments of Sappho's verse.[5]

Barney and Vivien in particular could not have failed to observe that despite its subject matter, *Bilitis* remained highly regarded, even after its inauthenticity was revealed. Many of the poems in *Bilitis* are torrid love poems from Bilitis to Mnasidika; nevertheless, the book was a great success. Love between women was evidently tolerable, even piquant, to the public taste if the lovers wore chitons. The fact that Louÿs was a male author writing on the subject might have provided a valuable lesson. As we have seen, Vivien and Barney originally did not publish in their full female identities. Even as late as 1909, Vivien decided to publish her translation of Sappho anonymously.

It was, however, initially through Barney that Vivien became acquainted with Sappho's work in an English translation by H. T. Wharton. Vivien was deeply impressed and conceived the desire to learn Greek so that she could read Sappho in the original. Barney was already studying Greek and French prosody with Charles-Brun, and he soon became Vivien's tutor as well. By 1902, after two years of study, Vivien knew Greek as well as her master. In "Our Secret Loves," Barney observed that Charles-Brun diligently taught them Greek while tactfully pretending not to notice the erotic content of their verse.[6]

Charles-Brun did not fail to point out to them that to duplicate the precise quantities of Sapphic verse in French was impossible:

> In spite of a docile appearance, *French* Sapphic meter is *further* from its Greek model than is our Alexandrine, which is taken from Homeric hexameter. If, indeed, Sapphic and Adonic meter or that of Horace and of Catullus is composed of a fixed number of syllables, and if substitution of the number of feet is forbidden, that does not make them consist any less of short and long syllables (just like the language to which they belong). These linguistic characteristics do not exist in French. That is why Classical meter is possibly susceptible to a direct transposition into English (as in the case of Swinburne's *Sapphics*), but not into our language.[7]

It might be pointed out, however, that Sapphic imitations are not particularly successful in English, either, primarily because the requisite line consists of eleven syllables, which contravenes the preference of English verse for a line consisting of an even number of syllables. The Sapphic stanza is a quatrain, the first three lines of which are scanned as follows:

$$| \acute{} \breve{} | / | / | \breve{} \breve{} | / | \breve{} | / | / | \breve{} |$$

and a following fourth line:

˘ ˘′ ˘
|/′ |/ /′ |

The fourth and eleventh syllables of the first three lines may be either trochees or spondees, as may be the last syllable of the fourth line.[8] The strain that this arrangement imposes even on one of its most accomplished English practitioners, Swinburne, is evident:

> ′ ˘   ′   ′   ′   ˘ ˘   ′   ˘   ′ ˘
> All the|night sleep|came not u|pon my eyelids,|
> ′   ˘   ′   ˘   ′   ˘ ˘   ′   ˘ ′ ˘
> Shed not|dew nor|shook nor un|closed a|feather,
> ′   ˘   ′   ˘   ′   ˘   ′   ˘ ′ ′ ˘
> Yet with|lips shut|close and with|eyes of|iron
>   ′   ˘   ˘   ′ ˘   ′
>   Stood and be|held me.[9]

French prosody, which is similarly syllabic rather than quantitative, prefers an even number of syllables: "In French poetics, the meter is divided into groups of two syllables, groups of four syllables, and into two successive groups of three syllables,"[10] so that the eleven-syllable Sapphic line sounds limping and forced in French.

Another difficulty in exact rendition lies in the caesura, which in French, as in English, must fall between words and may not interrupt a word, as it may in Greek.[11] Thus from the outset, both Barney and Vivien were encouraged by the very difficulties of translation itself to view Sappho as a source of inspiration rather than the object of scholarly veneration.

Yet these difficulties prevented neither woman from making a profound identification with Sappho. "Sappho represents . . . ," as Susan Gubar has demonstrated, "all the lost women of genius in literary history, especially all the lesbian artists whose work has been destroyed, sanitized, or heterosexualized in an attempt to evade what Elaine Marks identifies as 'lesbian intertextuality.'"[12] Barney sought to emulate Sappho by gathering around her a group of women who would be lovers as well as friends. Sappho "was the kind of woman she [Barney] wanted to be—a lover of beauty and the life of the senses, frankly sensual in her love of women and free to love as she chose."[13] Barney also used Sappho as a model for her own infidelities and claimed, for instance, that Sappho could be faithful to Atthis while loving others: "If we wish to capture the heart of harmony as epitomized by the traditions of Mytilene, then each new woman among us should become an element to fan our sacred fire, which we consecrate to the muses. She should not become the subject of jealousy."[14]

Because of Barney's infidelities, Vivien would come to see her more as the Atthis who eventually "betrayed" Sappho, rather than as Sappho herself. Vivien usually reserved this role for herself in her own work, although she casts herself as Atthis in "Atthis délaissée ("Atthis Abandoned"). Barney could also identify herself as Atthis.

Vivien identified so strongly with the Sapphic legend that at times she seemed to believe that she was the reincarnation of a follower of Sappho. In *A Woman Appeared to Me*, San Giovanni, her poetic alter ego, states:

> "If it is true . . . that the soul is reborn in several human forms, I was once born on Lesbos. I was only a sickly and graceless child, when an older companion led me into the temple where Sappho invoked the Goddess. I heard the 'Ode to Aphrodite.' Her incomparable voice rose up, more harmonious than water. . . . I swear, I once heard the 'Ode to Aphrodite.' The luminous memory will never fade through the years or even through the centuries."[15]

San Giovanni adds that she loved Sappho as a child, a love which continued into adulthood, but that, because of her homeliness and her lack of grace in speaking, that love was not returned.

Whether this sort of identification was simple fancy or the product of a more deeply held conviction, it is nevertheless interesting for what it suggests about Vivien's view of herself and about what relation she felt herself to have with the Sapphic tradition. Even when imagining herself back two thousand years in time, she picks the role of scorned lover. Such a choice, with its implicit notion of fatality, may explain to some degree her helplessness to end a relationship with Barney that was evidently unsuitable. As well, if Vivien genuinely believed that she was in fact the reincarnation of one of Sappho's disciples, she may have concluded that she had a kind of "divine right" to carry on Sappho's work in the modern age. Having known the "real Sappho," so to speak, she would now have the authority to interpret her life and work correctly. This "fantastic collaboration" with Sappho, as Gubar calls it "simultaneously heals the anxiety of authorship and links [her] . . . to an empowering literary history that [she] . . . could create in [her] . . . own image."[16] Several of her poems suggest this relationship to Sappho. In "Sonnet," in *Etudes and Preludes*, for example, Vivien first evokes the languorous beauty of Lesbos and then insists that she alone feels and recreates it because of her divine poetic right: "For the poet alone hears her return."[17] In "Psappha revit" ("Sappho Lives Again") in *At the Hour of Joined Hands*, Vivien sees

herself more as an heir of the Sapphic tradition because she has preserved
the rites established by Sappho:

> . . . Certaines d'entre nous ont conservé les
> rites
> De ce brûlant Lesbos doré comme un autel.
> Nous savons que l'amour est puissant et cruel,
> Et nos amantes ont les pieds blancs des
> Kharites.
> Nos corps sont pour leur corps un fraternel
> miroir.
> Nos compagnes, aux seins de neige printanière,
> Savent de quelle étrange et suave manière
> Psappha pliait naguère Atthis à son vouloir.

> . . . A few among us have preserved the rites
> Of burning Lesbos, as golden as an altar.
> We know that love is powerful and cruel,
> And our female lovers have the white feet of
> Kharites.
> For their bodies, our bodies form a sisterly
> mirror.
> Our companions, with breasts of spring snow,
> Know with what strange and suave manner
> Psappha once swayed Atthis to her wish.[18]

Whatever the basis of her fascination with Sappho, this influence led
Renée Vivien to create some of her best work, the work most devoid of
self-pity and morbidity: "This was the pure Sappho, who led her [Vivien]
down the magnificent path of poetry, far from the cult of martyrs and
relics, far from the haunted tombs, while dispersing the shadows which
hindered her from stretching her hands to the Sun."[19]

But beyond the simple question of identification lies the rather more
complex one of whom they were identifying with. As has already been
pointed out, the historical character of Sappho barely exists, except as an
idea. Depending on the taste and inclinations of the commentator, Sappho could be, and has been, seen as the passionate victim of heterosexual
desire, as Ovid portrays her,[20] the vicious corrupter of young womanhood, as Burton imagines her,[21] or, as Barney and Vivien evidently preferred, as the pure and semidivine center of a cult of poetry and female
love. In the fragments and in the accumulated tradition these writers
sought "facts" which would allow them to elevate what was commonly
viewed as decadent perversion to the status of a superior and purer kind of

love. Like any number of male homosexuals of their own and later days, they sought Classical authority as a defense of their sexual preferences. But beyond this "political" interest in Sappho, Barney and Vivien were motivated to find in her life and work some sort of guide to newer and finer forms of relationships among women, forms untainted by what they saw as masculinist notions of what was appropriate to women. Thus they took Sappho's "Ode to Aphrodite" and from it recreated a pagan cult with Aphrodite as its chief goddess. Vivien and Barney took Sappho's love of beauty and of women and placed these at the center of their works. They studied Sappho's relationships with her pupils and emulated the roles they thought Sappho had originated. They examined Sappho's morality and redefined the values of friendship, love, and the idea of an elite. Vivien was fascinated by Sappho's death and praised her suicide. In short, they did what they could to resurrect the Sapphic ideal in modern Paris, though it is unclear whether they were altogether aware that what they were in fact doing was less an act of resurrection than one of invention of new modes to suit the requirements of their own situation. Furthermore, while they sought to re-empower Sappho, they also empowered themselves by elevating an appropriate literary foremother.

Renée Vivien wrote four poetic plays about Sappho's life and Natalie Barney wrote one. Barney's play, "Equivoque" ("Ambiguity"), was probably written in 1905 or 1906 and was published in her book, *Acts and Entr'acts*, in 1910. In addition to the two plays which appear in *Evocations* (1903), "La Mort de Psappha," ("The Death of Psappha") and "Atthis Abandoned," Vivien wrote two other plays, "La Dogaresse" ("The Dogaressa") in *The Venus of the Blind*, 1903, and "Dans un verger" ("In an Orchard") in *Wakes*, 1908. In addition, she translated and elaborated upon Sapphic fragments in her *Sappho* (1903). Vivien's paraphrases and expansions of the fragments reveal a great deal of what she thought about Sappho as well as a great deal about Vivien herself. In *The Kitharedes* (1904), Vivien translated and elaborated certain minor Greek poets, among them Korinna, Myrtis, Telesippa, Eranna, Nossis, and Praxilla. Sappho appears throughout Vivien's poetry and is an element in her prose poems and tales, too. "Bona Dea" *(The Woman of the Wolf)* is, for example, a fictional reworking of the "Atthis, I loved you" fragment.

If Sappho were to serve successfully as the source of inspiration for a new cult of female creativity, it was necessary that the legends of her life be stripped of what Barney and Vivien considered to be vulgar male interpretations. Sappho could not, first of all, be permitted to commit suicide for the love of a man after having spent most of her life surrounded by so many lovely female disciples. Kerkolas, her husband, presented less of a problem to Barney, who perhaps saw him as the largely insignificant progenitor of Sappho's daugher, Cleïs; however, Vivien removed even him from her version of Sappho's life. Barney made it clear why Phaon had to go: "The great Sappho surrounded by her priestesses seemed a unique inspiration, and it was she that I most wished to emulate, at the same time rejecting the legend of Phaon as unworthy of her and her cult."[22]

In "Ambiguity" Barney recreated the story to her liking. At the beginning of the play, all of Sappho's disciples believe that she is suffering from jealousy because her lover Phaon is marrying Timas. Sappho watches the ceremony and then, promising to haunt the newly-wedded pair, drops the poems she has just completed and leaps off the cliffs into the sea. Gorgo and Eranna read the verses, which make it clear that Sappho loved *Timas*, not Phaon. At the end, Timas is left alone at the altar. The others have been persuaded by a visitor that Sappho would not want them to mourn, and Timas "for the last time clasps the pearls, the harp and the parchment that Sappho has left on the altar, and then takes the path which leads to the Sea,"[23] thus following Sappho to her death. In this play, Barney challenges the stubbornly reiterated notion of Sappho's death by maintaining that it arose out of a predictable heterosexual misconception. If Sappho did kill herself for love, in Barney's view, she was far more likely to have done so for the love of a woman than for a man. This play, incidentally, incorporates translations of sixteen Sapphic fragments, the originals of which are appended to the play. In yet another play, this one unpublished, Aphrodite is heard firmly to dismiss the story of Phaon as "a legend, my child, a legend . . . a man's legend."[24]

Renée Vivien also rejects the story of Phaon and that of Kerkolas as well. In *A Woman Appeared to Me*, Vally asks San Giovanni: " 'Haven't they invented the legend of an idiotic infatuation for the swell Phaon, a legend whose stupidity is equalled only by its lack of historic truth? And finally, haven't they almost universally adopted a hypothesis of a marriage that the comic writers of Athens invented to ridicule her?' "[25] San Giovanni explains Kerkolas away on linguistic evidence:

> "According to Suidas, this supposed husband . . . would have left the island of Andros in search of a wife. But the name of the husband, Kerkolas, which means 'he who uses a pen,' as well as that of his country sufficiently indicates the kind of abject joke which gave birth to them. Besides, it was not at all the custom of the Greeks to leave their city with the intention of marrying a foreigner."[26]

This passage gives some indication of the seriousness with which Renée Vivien took both her studies of Greek and her task of revealing the true meaning of the life of Sappho.

In her tales and stories also, Vivien consistently expresses her idea of Sappho as having been wholly untouched by heterosexual involvement. In "La Sirène muette" ("The Mute Siren") in *Fogs of the Fjords,* for example, one of the Sirens is silent. When the others demand the reason she does not sing, she informs them that it is because Sappho has just killed herself. But the Siren makes it clear that it was for Atthis, not Phaon, that Sappho leaped to her death; she reports her final words: *"Atthis, I used to love you. . . ."*[27]

In her study of Sappho, Edith Mora noted that Vivien, along with Lucie Delarue-Mardrus and others, had resurrected Sappho as a Lesbian, though Mora implied this was a negative development, which destroyed Sappho's "moral reputation."[28] She failed to realize that Barney apparently had quite a role in Sappho's coming out, as it were. Furthermore, as Monique Wittig and Sande Zeig implied when they left a blank page for the entry "Sappho" in their *Lesbian Peoples: Material for a Dictionary,*[29] Sappho is so mythical that many characteristics may be attributed to her. Therefore, it is equally as valid to assume her Lesbianism as her heterosexuality. In fact, it seems ironic that so many critics should try to purify a historical figure whose work was most likely destroyed by the Christians for its sexual deviancy as well as its paganism.

In any event, Vivien, in particular, went further than restructuring Sappho's sex life: She turned as well to the reinterpretation of Sappho's death. Vivien agreed with Barney that Sappho had to die for the love of a woman. In "The Death of Psappha," the clear indication is that Atthis caused Sappho's suicide. In the beginning of the play, one of Sappho's disciples, Eranna of Telos, is singing in front of Sappho's school: " 'I recall the crease of her closed lids, / The flower of her eyes, the sob of her voice, / And I weep for Atthis, whom I once loved / In the shade of the roses. . . .' "[30] The quotation marks indicate that Eranna is not speaking in her own voice but is quoting Sappho, citing indeed that fragment to which Vivien obsessively returned and which seems to have been the expression of her mourning for the loss of her relationship with Barney.

Sappho recalls her second ode to Aphrodite: " *'Why sob out my name! What beauty, Psappha, resists you?'* "[31] Aphrodite had promised Sappho that no one would be able to resist her charms, but now the goddess has turned against her and removed her protection: "Thy venom corrupts the day's smile, / Goddess, and withers my humiliated flesh, / Thou who were once my radiant help, / My swift ally."[32] The implication is that Aphrodite, who helped Sappho win the love of Atthis, has now permitted Atthis to fall out of love with her. The goddess who was Sappho's protector has now apparently also betrayed her. It is also evident that the "Beauty" for whom Sappho suffers is a woman. This is not surprising, since Atthis represents Barney's equivalent in Vivien's work: It is she, not Timas, as Barney would have it, for whom Sappho suffers.

In a more important transformation of the biography, several of Sappho's disciples—Gurinno, Eranna, Atthis, Damophyla, and Gorgo (here a disciple, not a rival)—are nearby during her final agony and leap. They describe Sappho's offstage death, but do nothing to prevent it. In fact, they experience it vicariously, drinking in "the voluptuousness of death . . . in the air."[33] And then, on the authority of another of Vivien's favorite fragments, they celebrate her death: "Sing! You must fill with rhythm and roses / The house of the poet where mourning may not enter."[34]

What is particularly noteworthy about this version of Sappho's story is that Vivien arranges matters so that the disciples could prevent the death of Sappho but *choose not to*. Neither tradition nor Barney concur with this interpretation, but it was one wholly consistent with Vivien's personal cult of death.

Vivien sought not merely to deliver Sappho from heterosexuality, but also to elevate her to the status of goddess. She felt that the very name by which Sappho is commonly known was a bourgeois denigration of her ideal, and preferred Sappho's own Aeolic spelling, *Psappha*. In *A Woman Appeared to Me* Vally complains of the inadequacy of the name "Sappho": " 'They have even misrepresented her divine name, her sonorous and gentle name—Psappha—for which they have substituted the colorless designation—Sappho," sighed Vally. "Sappho! That imperiously suggests mediocre statues and trite verse by means of which the bourgeois mobs perpetuate the greatest female figure who ever dazzled the Universe.' "[35] Thus the first step in elevating Sappho was to reclaim for her her own name. The power to name or to rename, was one of Vivien's most potent tools, as it has been for other feminist authors. Seventy years before Mary Daly noted that "women have had the power of *naming* stolen from us,"[36] Vivien reinstated Sappho's ancient name as a signal that the figure which appears in Vivien's work is not to be confused with the conventional Sappho, but is the "real," divine Psappha, at last restored to her rightful place as divinity.

The second step in the deification of Sappho was to redefine her essence through the praise bestowed on her by the characters in the various works describing her life. Both Barney and Vivien used this approach, but in each case, the Sappho who emerges from their praise bears a rather marked resemblance to Barney or Vivien rather than to a jointly-shared concept of the "real" Sappho. In "Gentle Rivalries," which appears in *Five Short Greek Dialogues*, Barney has Eranna celebrate Sappho:

"She is compelling as are all those who have followed their true nature. She is compelling as are all those who have dared to live. She is as compelling as Destiny herself. . . . She is sublime, young, gentle, and formidable. Sappho is the flame which at the same time lights and destroys. Her approach dazzles and her flight consoles. . . ."[37]

Like Barney's own, Sappho's main achievement is portrayed as her life. In "Ambiguity," Gorgo proclaims: "Your life is your most beautiful poem / Your eternal masterpiece / Is yourself."[38] Considering that by the time she wrote this play, Barney was quite well-established in her habits, it seems reasonable to presume that she here celebrates in Sappho what is in fact an image of herself.

Vivien was no less apt to recreate Sappho in her own image; if anything, she was even more prone to do so. Vivien's Sappho seems to be suffering from an advanced case of *mal du siècle* as she speaks of her "ardent suffering" in a poem based on the fragment in which Sappho wonders if she will be remembered in the future. In the next fragment, Vivien adds the words, "ardent anguish." Neither expression has any equivalent in Sappho's sparse lines. As Le Dantec remarks, however musical and sincere Vivien's version of Sappho might be, she fills Sappho with Baudelairean spleen, thus failing to recapture Sappho's serene soul.[39] But as Gubar suggests, Vivien might be reclaiming Decadence as "fundamentally a lesbian . . . tradition."[40] In "In an Orchard," Sappho's disciples rail bitterly against Aphrodite, who has taken away their leader: "Fickle Aphrodite, implacable Immortal! / Thou sprang from the sea, perilous as she. / The waves under thy feet broke into sobs. / Bitter, thou surged from the bitter depths."[41] In the original, Sappho cajoles the goddess and pleads with her, but neither she nor her disciples curse the divinity in this rather more modern manner.

Although Barney and Vivien were not in complete accord concerning the precise qualities to be attributed to Sappho, they did concur that her importance transcended ordinary literary influence; neither was willing to settle for a Sappho who was a mere mortal. At times, Vivien treats Sappho as if she were a muse: "With thy harmonious breath, / Inspire us, Psappha!"[42] Elsewhere, she is imagined as an immortal, lodged in Hades, and able to hear Vivien's songs and prayers, but lacking identifiable power: "O Lesbos, I am dear to Immortal Psappha. / In Hades, she hears my fleeting harmonies / And the virgin of my desire seems lovely to her. / She smiles from within the cloud of the Dead. . . ."[43] In other places, however, Sappho is portrayed as a goddess and is called a "Divinity with temples of orange trees."[44] Vivien sees herself in the role of Sappho's priestess, and her goddess has the power to protect her in love. In other words, the Greek poetess takes over some of the functions of Aphrodite: "Know . . . that Psappha, reclining among the Lethean lotuses, smiles when I invoke her and extends her protection over my love affairs because I am her Priestess."[45] Thus, Vivien empowers herself as a woman and as a poet while she empowers Sappho as a deity.

As Sappho's priestess, Vivien's task is to destroy the myths and lies about her and to relight the flames at her abandoned altars, to resurrect the Sapphic virtues, morality, and love: "I have never listened to those who lie . . . / And, pious disciple, at thy broken altar, / I have relighted the expiring ardor of the flames."[46]

If to Barney, Sappho served primarily as authorization and justification for an attitude toward life and art which she already held, to Vivien, Sappho took on a quasi-religious significance so pervasive that phrases, lines, and entire Sapphic fragments persistently, even obsessively, appear over and over again throughout her work.

As has been previously remarked, both Barney and Vivien retained a streak of American pragmatism which demanded that theory be actualized whenever an opportunity presented itself. Thus, it seemed logical and reasonable to both writers to attempt to rekindle the Sapphic flame not merely in verse, but in actuality, not only in Paris, but eventually on Lesbos itself. As early as the end of 1900 or the beginning of 1901, they wrote to a young English poet, Olive Custance, proposing that they form a Sapphic circle in Paris. Although Barney's biographer, George Wickes, doubts that Barney was altogether serious in making this proposal,[47] there is no reason to assume that she was any less serious about it than she was about her later attempt to found a women's colony on Lesbos, or to establish an Academy of Women. At any rate, Olive Custance certainly took them seriously, for she joined them in Paris in the spring of 1901.

In 1904, Barney and Vivien decided to extend their commitment to the Sapphic ideal by making a voyage to Lesbos. They set out with minds filled with images of a Greece which they had at least partially built on the foundations of Sapphic verse. As Barney wrote in a journal entry, "It seemed to me that we were living in a distant country about six centuries before Christ, a divinely honest era when modesty was immodesty, when perverse things, far from being calumnious, were joyous and simple."[48]

Predictably, both were distressed by the modern reality, which had little to do with the Greece of their dreams. They were greeted on Lesbos by blaring music; Barney was unimpressed by the faces of contemporary Greek women; Vivien could not understand modern Greek. In a letter to her mother, Barney expressed her disappointment: She complained that the Greeks "must have been in reality horrid, dirty people—the sight of so many tarnished feet quite ruins our illusions about the Greeks—But these as Dr. [J. C.] Mardrus says are 'Greeks made in Germany' so that one cannot really judge them by what the real ones may have looked like."[49] Not untypically, the Greeks before her eyes on Lesbos were not "real." The real ones, like the real Sappho, glowed in the imagination. Despite the music and the dirt, the women bought two houses in My-tilene and decided to remain to establish their Sapphic school of poetry. Lesbos, for all its superficial corruption, remained sacred soil. Though Vivien left the island to be reunited with the Baroness de Zuylen, it was to remain the place of her greatest happiness.

Like Monique Wittig more than half a century later, Barney and Vivien saw in Lesbos the luminous center of a new, feminized religion. The conception of Lesbos that Wittig expresses in *The Lesbian Body* is strik-ingly close to that of Barney and Vivien: ". . . farewell black continent of misery and suffering farewell ancient cities we are embarking for the shining radiant isles and for the green Cytheras, for the dark and gilded Lesbos."[50] The "Cythera" here referred to is the island traditionally asso-ciated with Aphrodite. Wittig never mentions Aphrodite's name in her text, evidently because she is synthesizing numerous goddesses. How-ever, Barney and Vivien, on the authority, no doubt, of Sappho's "Ode," made a considerable effort to reclaim the goddess for the religion of women. This effort at reclamation required that those elements of the Aphrodite tradition which connect her with heterosexual passion be reinterpreted or ignored, just as Kerkolas and Phaon were transformed in Barney's and Vivien's versions of the life of Sappho.

Barney's and Vivien's evocations of Aphrodite have been generally at-tributed by their biographers to a vaguely-defined "paganism," which was fashionable in avant-garde circles of their period. But in the case of Barney and Vivien, the term is probably somewhat misleading, for they were selective in their worship of ancient deities, ignoring Dionysus and Pan, the favorite faun of their male contemporaries, in favor of a few female figures. The male gods who appeared in their work existed primarily to embody negative principles, not as objects of adoration. Thus a more appropriate term than paganism might be "goddess-worshippers," for Barney and Vivien were devoted to the cult of the Great Mother. She was represented for them primarily by Aphrodite, but to a lesser degree also by Artemis, Lilith, and Hekate, as well as the Virgin Mary, all of whom contained one or more aspects of the Great Mother.[51]

Barney and Vivien were developing their ideas about feminine religion at about the same time that the worship of the primordial goddess was becoming a topic of considerable intellectual interest, partly as a result of the publication of Sir James Frazer's *The Golden Bough* in 1890. Frazer's work was the object of particular controversy because of the parallels it drew between details of the story of Christ and elements of the worship of the Great Goddess as well as because of its identification of the Virgin Mary with aspects of the ancient Moon Goddess. Whether Barney and Vivien had direct knowledge of Frazer's monumental study or whether they had become aware of its contents through articles and reviews is unclear, but certainly their work demonstrates a familiarity with the figure and with the details of the worship of the Mother Goddess. Both Barney and Vivien often refer to her simply as "the goddess." Vivien dreamed of restoring her cult. In *A Woman Appeared to Me*, San Giovanni, who speaks for Vivien, states: " 'I would have liked to found a religion or reestablish a very ancient and very obscurely wise cult—the primitive cult of the Mother Goddess, who once upon a time conceived Space and gave birth to Eternity.' "[52]

In Vivien's work, the Mother Goddess appears as Bona Dea as well, also called Fauna. The worship of Bona Dea was "a very ancient cult. . . . In her worship no man might be present, no myrtle might be used, and also no wine. . . . Bona Dea was the wife, or the daughter, of Faunus, and renowned for her chastity."[53] Her chaste nature, as well as the strict elimination of men from her service, obviously appealed to Barney and Vivien, and these two characteristics were of course retained in their literary representations of her. The most significant treatment of Bona Dea appears in a prose poem of that name in Vivien's collection of short pieces, *The Woman of the Wolf.* Here, the goddess so abhors men that their very portraits must be veiled lest they offend her; nevertheless, she is portrayed as simple, gentle, chaste, and forgiving. It is she who makes the flowers grow.

For feminist and Lesbian writers, the Greek goddess most commonly invoked is Artemis, goddess of the moon, the chaste huntress who wreaks a terrible vengeance on those males who violate her precincts. For instance, in Colette's *The Vagabond*, the Baths of Diana in Nîmes have a great impact on Renée's decision not to marry Max.[54] We might expect that Barney and Vivien too would prefer the Virgin-aspect of the triple Goddess, but instead we find that it is Aphrodite who figures prominently in their work. The choice is less surprising, however, in view of the immense importance they placed on the devotion of women elevated into a religion of love. In this context, Aphrodite, the goddess of love, makes considerable sense.

Aphrodite is the primary goddess mentioned in the work of Sappho, particularly in her longest extant poem, the "Ode to Aphrodite," in which Sappho petitions Aphrodite to intervene on her behalf as she has done several times in the past:

> then, blissful one,
>
> smiling your immortal smile
> you asked, What ailed me now that
> made me call you again? What
>
> was it that my distracted
> heart most wanted? . . .
>
> "Who, Sappho, is
> unfair to you? For let her
> run, she will soon run after;
>
> "if she won't accept gifts, she
> will one day give them; and if
> she won't love you—she soon will
>
> "love, although unwillingly. . . .[55]

This poem, in which Sappho invokes Aphrodite in a specifically homoerotic context, would have provided Barney and Vivien with support for their belief that Aphrodite, like Sappho herself, might be dissociated from her heterosexual associations and reclaimed for an exclusively female religion. Because of this poem and other fragments in which Sappho makes similar appeals to the goddess (see particularly fragments 37 and 42), Barney imagined a special connection between Aphrodite and Lesbos, although she is more conventionally connected with Cyprus. Barney calls Lesbos the "sister of Aphrodite," and without hesitation names Lesbos as the new center of Aphrodite's cult.[56]

The frequency with which Sappho invokes the name of Aphrodite is probably sufficient to explain the importance of that goddess to Barney and Vivien, but certain aspects of her legend made her attractive in other ways as well. In particular, her origin was, from Barney and Vivien's point of view, "purer" than that of Artemis or Athena, for Aphrodite was ocean-born; that is, she arose from a purely "feminine" source.[57] Although her conception may have had some help from Uranus' severed member, she was not, like Artemis, the daughter of Zeus, nor did she, like Athena, spring from her father's head.

Although Artemis may not appear directly in the poetry of Vivien, images of the moon abound. Certainly Vivien shared a fondness for Verlaine's sad and lovely moonlight, but for Vivien it was more than the romantic ambiguity of moonlight which made her prefer its pallor to the broad light of day. For Vivien, as for many other women poets, the moon "presages change . . . [and] her phases imitate the rhythms of feminine time. . . ."[58] Though this concept is hardly new and is found in all mythologies, Vivien believed that she had a somewhat novel and more intimate connection with the moon than could her male counterparts. Vivien passionately reclaimed the moon and, in so doing, her own heritage: "For the night is ours as the day belongs to others."[59] The masculine gender of the French word for *day ("jour")* carries the suggestion that the "others" are likewise masculine.

Renée Vivien in particular celebrated ancient cults in which the moon was worshipped. In *A Woman Appeared to Me*, Vally claims that in another life, she told the rest of the village that the moon was rising: " 'And all those to whom I announced the great news looked at the sky and rejoiced to see on the horizon the amber light which precedes the Moon.' "[60] This passage not only suggests a belief in reincarnation, but also evokes an historical past in which the rising of the moon was greeted as an event of religious significance.

In addition, Vivien identified with those later moon-worshippers, the witches. In "Enseignement" ("Education"), Vivien states that the witches were unmoved by the apparent triumph of the sun: "Little does it matter to them if, later, finally conquered / By the powers of day, their living music / Extinguished, like the weak call of the conquered. . . ."[61]

In this poem, Vivien, as later feminists were to do, identifies with the witches as victims of persecution because of their supposed "abnormality." Her insistence that "they have the right to exist and to be born . . ."[62] makes it clear that she identifies with them because of her own Lesbianism and persecution by a majority which neither understands her nor will allow her to pursue her own beliefs in peace.

But it was not simply as victims of patriarchal power that the witches appealed to Barney and Vivien. To them, as to Baudelaire and Mallarmé, the witches had a transformational power, the power to alter substance through magic arising out of their willingness to evoke the dark side of the human psyche. Barney called the moon "the goddess of evil."[63] Vivien admired the magical powers of the witches, those "possessing the secret of love potions and charms."[64] Her "Flowers of Séléné," one of the names of the moon-as-goddess, could easily be the "Flowers of Evil" of Baudelaire. This attraction to the mysticism of moonlight, to the power of the nonrational, led Vivien, as it had Baudelaire, to a generalized mysticism and later to a preoccupation with certain aspects of Roman Catholicism.

The aspect of the moon-goddess Vivien and Barney worshipped was that which they associated with Aphrodite, not Artemis, despite the latter's traditional association with the moon. This magical goddess is borrowed from Baudelaire's black mistress of the night:

> Le feuillage s'écarte en des plis de rideaux
> Devant la Vénus des Aveugles, noire
> Sous la majesté de ses noirs bandeaux.
> Le temple a des murs d'ébène et d'ivoire
> Et le sanctuaire est la nuit des nuits. . . .

> The foliage parts like the folds of curtains
> Before the Venus of the Blind, black
> Under the majesty of her black blindfold.
> The temple's walls are made of ebony and
>   ivory
> And the sanctuary is the night of
>   nights. . . .[65]

This is not the conventional Aphrodite of Greek myth, light, capricious, flirtatious, and sometimes dangerous. Nor is she even Sappho's Aphrodite, a personal deity willing to intervene in Sappho's affairs of the heart. This Aphrodite is the ruler of the night, mysterious and cruel, and her followers are blind, or blinded, like Mozart's Queen of the Night. Unlike the usual representation of Aphrodite, but like the women Barney and Vivien adored—as we shall see in the following chapter—she is cold and remote: "Virgin, she loves snow in the woods."[66] And like those same women, she is slightly decadent: "perverse and chaste at the same time."[67] Vivien presents the qualities of this perverse, negative Aphrodite in the beginning of her play, "The Death of Psappha," when the chorus enters, chanting:

> Aphrodita changeante, implacable Immortelle,
> Tu jaillis de la mer, périlleuse comme elle.
> La vague sous tes pas se brisait en sanglots.
> Amère, tu surgis des profondeurs amères,
> Apportant dans tes mains l'angoisse et les
>   chimères,
> Ondoyante, insondable et perfide. . . .
>
> Fickle Aphrodite, implacable Immortal,
> Thou sprang from the sea as perilous as she.
> The waves under thy feet broke into sobs.
> Bitter, thou sprang from the bitter depths,
> Carrying agony and nightmares in thy hands,
> Undulating, unfathomable and perfidious. . . ."[68]

Here we see neither the Classical Aphrodite nor quite the goddess of the Symbolists and Decadents, as in Mallarmé's "Hérodiade." Her virginity and cold chastity are attributes of feminine strength, which permit her to reject men firmly and authoritatively.

Nevertheless, aspects of this vision of Aphrodite would be congenial to the Symbolists. She is an indoor goddess. Her temple is dark and cloistral, much like Vivien's own apartment. Aphrodite and her worshippers "live in a weary dream, lonely / As the moon. . . ."[69] Clearly, she and her followers do not belong to the realm of ordinary beings. They live apart, preoccupied not with the pressing realities of everyday existence, but captivated by a dream of death.

Barney and Vivien's Aphrodite must be absolutely and unquestionably followed. She is never wrong, even when she is unreasoning, perverse, and cruel. If Aphrodite torments her lovers, it is because love itself is cruel: She herself must never be blamed.[70] For example, Sappho, in "The Mute Siren," cannot blame Aphrodite, though she has led her to destruction: "For even in her supreme despair, she could not curse the Goddess, who once heaped on her so many bitter joys."[71]

As we shall see, the Aphrodite portrayed by Vivien and Barney is the goddess of the religion of love, a goddess who evidences the same profound dualism of that religion. To classify Barney and Vivien as neo-pagans is to miss the point of their goddess-worship, for their Aphrodite does everything she can to prevent a pagan sensuality. She withdraws in dismay from the prospect of a blissful, guiltless, sensual union and demands a rigorous chastity.

The lower, sensual plane of love belongs to Eros. If Aphrodite represents that higher, pure, asexual gynandrous level to which Barney and Vivien aspire, Eros represents the lower, erotic, masculine plane. Barney stated this dichotomy outright in her introduction to "The Mystery of Psyche": ". . . The spherical lamp of Aphro[ditc] represents the celestial plane, and the lamp of Eros, the terrestrial plane."[72] Eros must be introduced, therefore, to provide the tension between the feminine ideal Vivien and Barney sought and the masculine reality they scrupulously tried to avoid. In her play, "The Mystery of Psyche," Barney sets up the duality between Eros and Aphrodite in an alarmingly simplistic fashion. Both Eros and Aphrodite are in love with the same woman, Psyche. Whereas Eros wants to possess her body, Aphrodite wishes to elevate Psyche's soul. In his quest, Eros lists as his goals: "to possess, . . . lock up, . . . know sexually, . . . dominate." For Aphrodite, the list is rather different: "to experience, . . . liberate, . . . discover, . . . serve."[73] In a reference to the origins of these ideals, Aphrodite notes that she and Eros have created two distinct religions of love: "the aphrodisial and the erotic." She represents intense passion; Eros embodies carnal sensuality. Ultimately, he is all men, for, according to Barney, all men are symbolically his father.[74]

Since both Aphrodite and Eros are in love with a woman, Aphrodite evidently represents a Lesbian principle, while Eros remains associated with heterosexuality. In other respects, however, Eros in this play is unconventionally conceived. He is neither the playful Cupid who ambushes unwary lovers with the arrows of love, nor even the son of the Great Goddess. Instead, he resembles a satyr, implacably sensual. Vivien also emphasizes this interpretation, for she describes Eros' sexuality, as she does all heterosexual copulation, as *souillure* ("dirt").[75] Like the devil, he tempts women to commit the sins of the flesh and creates the anguish of desire. Although, like Aphrodite, he is "fatal, bitter and gentle," and causes "anguish,"[76] his is the suffering of the flesh, while she precipitates the pain of chaste love. In Vivien's final treatment of the death of Sappho (1908), she blames Eros for Sappho's despair; however, Sappho is not a guiltless victim of implacable Eros, for it was she who fell into the abyss of the sensual, thus sealing her fate.[77]

Just as the Sappho envisioned and projected by Barney and Vivien was a figure constructed from selected details which suited their programmatic needs, their Eros and Aphrodite are also gods of their own making. As one of Barney's characters, Deïs, proclaims, " 'I create / all of my own gods. . . .' "[78] Elsewhere, Barney asked, "Why resurrect gods when new gods await creation?"[79] Nevertheless, these gods were not so much newly created as suitably edited versions of the old ones. In fact, they borrowed certain of the legends of the Great Goddess, added those mythic aspects of Aphrodite which they found appropriate, and eliminated those qualities which were offensive to their vision in order to find for themselves a goddess who might serve as the holy center of their religion of love. The qualities which Aphrodite was made to shed were transferred to her son, Eros, who became the repository of all other evil traits—in short, the devil to oppose their goddess.

Thus the presumptive paganism of Barney and Vivien appears on closer examination to be a goddess-centered version of Christian dualism. Both Barney and Vivien found themselves unavoidably reproducing the dualism of Chrétien de Troyes and certain of the Symbolists, inadvertently carrying forward a truly masculine inheritance. Although daring to the degree that the new religion was firmly centered on the worship and service of women, it carried with it a profound conceptual flaw, which prevented it from breaking free of the burden of Symbolism and Christianity to become the new ideology which Barney and Vivien had hoped to create.

V.

THE RELIGION OF LOVE

In Barney's and Vivien's quests for a continuing female tradition, it was not surprising that both should turn to the worship of the Virgin Mary and to the courtly love tradition, both of which offered provocative examples of the persistence of the primacy of the female principle. But the heterosexual and patriarchal elements in these traditions ran counter to the sensuous egalitarianism implicit in their "paganism." Particularly in Renée Vivien's case, these elements reinforced a tendency toward a rarefied purity that was difficult to reconcile absolutely with her otherwise wholehearted acceptance of the religion of Sappho.

A consideration of the use to which this material was put by both Barney and Vivien in their poems and prose provides certain insights into the complexities of their literary relationship. In general Barney was the theoretician of the two and Vivien found the means and the language to work out the ideas in poetry and prose. In the case of this particularly significant body of material, however, it would appear that Barney, under the influence of Vivien's natural mysticism, was encouraged to enlarge her more characteristically realistic and pragmatic attitude toward experience to include a recognition of the legitimacy of spiritual aspiration. Certainly, the poetry she wrote during her association with Renée Vivien and immediately following her death demonstrates a more intense concern with religion and mystical concepts than we find in her later work.

It was the Virgin Mary's similarities to the Great Goddess which initially attracted both writers to this Christian model. The resemblance was by no means lost on the Catholic Church itself, which had seized on the opportunity provided by the worship of Mary to assimilate local pagan practices into orthodox Christianity. In the cult of the Virgin, May is Mary's month; the name of the month is derived from Maia, a nymph first identified with Diana and then with Bona Dea,[1] a goddess of the earth, whose cult Vivien celebrates in a story of the same name.

But the May festivities which the Church associated with the worship of Mary are fertility rites now paradoxically attached to a Virgin, an evident contradiction which can be resolved only by faith. By establishing the Virgin as a central model for womanhood, the Catholic Church erects an unattainable ideal which confirms the believer in her sense of unworthiness and the need for the solace of the Church itself. Yet chastity was an essential component in generating a female figure of enormous power. The ancient matriarchists had recognized virginity as an expression of absolute female autonomy, as the multiplication of virgin goddesses in various pre-Christian mythologies attests. But these goddesses were by no means sexually abstemious.[2] Even Hera, wife of Zeus and mother of many, had her maidenhead magically restored in an annual ritual.[3] The mystical virginity of Mary continues this ancient tradition, but since the notion of the aloof, independent, and wholly autonomous female did not confirm to Pauline ideas of the appropriate role for the Christian woman, her virginity rapidly became a literal one, with all the consequent contradictions which have marked developing Christian attitudes.[4] All Christians have inherited this conflict, and Barney and Vivien were no exceptions, even if their relation to Christianity was by no means orthodox. When both writers attempted to redeem Mary for a religion of love, they wanted her to be at once absolutely chaste and the symbolic center of a religion which had a strong component of Lesbian sexuality. These aspects were not easy to reconcile.

This paradox may account for the fact that the image of the Madonna projected in Vivien's poetry and prose was frequently a decadent one so that she became a goddess of desire and fever as well as a source of purity and light. She made Mary an indoor goddess, worshipped in darkened temples, or the perverse embodiment of all that was vile. In *A Woman Appeared to Me*, the narrator enters a church during a pilgrimage in Spain: "Little by little, I could make out the cruel pallor of the Madonna of the Plague. In her stagnant eyes reflections of dead waters turned azure and green. Paludal breaths emanated from the tormented folds of her dress. Her face was tumultuous like a delirious vision."[5]

When, in Vivien's verse, the symbol of the Virgin is wrenched from its social context, the potential for a radical movement of significance emerges. "The Holy Virgin" transformed into "the Madonna of the Plague" may be, and is, as foul as she is pure. One particularly strongly negative image is that of "Our Lady of Fever," in a poem introducing the second volume of Vivien's collected works—a position which reinforces the poem's importance:

> Ton haleine fétide a corrompu la ville . . .
> Un vert de gangrène, un vert de poison
> Grouille, et la nuit rampe ainsi qu'un
> > reptile.
> La foule redit en chœur l'oraison,
> Délire fervent qui brûle les lèvres,
> Frisson glacial parmi les sueurs,
> Vers ta lividité, Notre-Dame des Fièvres!
>
> Your fetid breath corrupted the city . . .
> A gangrene green, a poisonous green
> Is swarming, and the night crawls like a
> > reptile.
> In unison the crowd repeats the prayer,
> The fervent delirium that burns their lips,
> A glacial shiver among the sweat,
> Towards your lividness, Our Lady of the
> > Fevers![6]

The corrupt Madonna of the night, the Madonna of the ill and feverish, the "Madonna of the pest-ridden," all these are images that belong not to the Church but to the Decadents. The Madonna, usually clad in pure white and the blue of heaven, has become a sickly green. Delirium, not salvation, is what she inspires. This is surely the Madonna of a Baudelaire, not the heavenly lady of the Church.

The irreconcilability of literal virginity with a "pagan" pleasure in the joys of the flesh unquestionably reinforced Renée Vivien's increasing tendency toward mysticism. A mystical theme runs throughout her work from the 1902 *Ashes and Dust* to the last posthumous volume. The source for this mysticism is again more Baudelairean than Catholic. Aside from the direct influences of Baudelaire and the Decadents, what attracted her in particular to the nonrational aspect of Christianity was the sensuality of ritual, which had been rigidly excluded from the austere and rational Protestantism with which both she and Barney had grown up. Indeed, perhaps it was the recognition of the female principle that attracted both Barney and Vivien to Catholic ritual. As Barney once remarked: "The Holy Virgin was the first Catholic concession to feminism."[7]

This fascination with Catholic ritual was shared by a large number of Lesbian writers in the early years of this century, among whom were Radclyffe Hall and Una Troubridge. To a contemporary Lesbian critic, Bertha Harris, this absorption in ritual appears destructive:

> Catholicism was one of the major weapons used [by the patriarchy] in the
> psychological destruction of these women. Seduced by the secretiveness of
> the ritual, by the incense, color, and most particularly, by the nature of its
> death-wishing drama, most of these women succumbed to its invid-
> iousness at some point in their lives. . . .[8]

But to dismiss this element in Vivien's thought as a kind of weakness of
will or failure of nerve is to miss the point. The struggle to redeem from
centuries of patriarchy those kernels of remembrance of the primacy of
the female principle had to be undertaken against enormous odds. It is a
struggle which continues today in the writing of women like Monique
Wittig, Merlin Stone, and Mary Daly, but now it is undertaken within the
context of a large and vital feminist movement in which such ideas are
welcome and congenial. At the turn of the century when such an undertaking could only be generally regarded as eccentric or bizarre, Barney
and Vivien were the only two women authors writing in the hope of
resurrecting Mary as an incarnation of the Goddess. It is hardly surprising, therefore, that Vivien, in particular, may have been overwhelmed by
the weight of a tradition she was attempting almost single-handedly to
shift.

It was both Vivien's intense involvement with Catholicism and her
mysticism which most sharply differentiate her from Natalie Barney.
Although Barney was capable, even anxious, to admit some element of
transcendence into her work, she remained firmly committed to the
principle of earthly survival: "I strongly felt that to live is more difficult
than to die. In order to die, all you have to do is to let go. It's very
simple."[9] Further, as she remarks in a poem for Renée Vivien in her
unpublished memoirs, it is more difficult to love than to die.[10] For Vivien,
however, the alienation she experienced as a product of her literary
inheritance and, existentially, as a Lesbian, inexorably drew her toward an
obsession with the figure of the suffering Christ, an identification impossible to Barney, who could consider no male figure, regardless of his
attractiveness, an adequate expression of her female-identified spirit.
Even on her Passy tombstone, Barney had inscribed the audacious words
insisting that "she was the Amazon."

Vivien's identification with Christ was far from complete. It is the
alienation which attracted her, not the spirit of forgiveness. She describes
herself not as one whom ". . . the crowd celebrates / But one whom it
hates. . . ."[11] Like Christ, she sees herself nailed to the cross: "For a long
time, I was nailed to the cross, / And some women, seeing that I was

suffering, laughed. / Then, some men took mud in their hands / Which splattered my temples and my cheek."[12]

But having imagined herself as the object of the scorn and hostility of the crowd, male and female alike, unlike Christ, she cannot forgive; instead, "Silently, I learned to hate them."[13] Nor does her rejection fill her with zeal for justification or for the conversion of the masses. Instead, she announces that her work is reserved for those few who can comprehend it. Thus, it is not the resurrected Christ who draws Vivien, but the rejected and despised figure, forever fixed to his cross in the midst of an uncaring world. Vivien at once welcomes rejection as an affirmation of her own separateness and special character, and yearns for death as a release from suffering and pain.

From a strictly literary viewpoint, she is the lover of death and enemy of life, for the sacred leap to death holds the promise of blissful union with the beloved mistress of the religion of love. Like Villiers de l'Isle-Adam's Axël and Sara, Vivien and her lover will be united in death as they never could be in life, tenderly and purely. She was not the only Lesbian to subscribe to such a belief. Radclyffe Hall converted to Catholicism partly in the hope of being united in heaven with her former lover, Mabel Veronica Batten ("Ladye"), and with Lady Una Troubridge. Like Hall and Troubridge, Vivien conveniently overlooked the Church's negative teachings about homosexuality, which would exclude her from a Catholic heaven altogether. Like many Catholic Lesbians today, some of whom remain sisters in the Church, the Catholic Lesbians of Paris glossed over their paradoxical behavior or arrived at a private interpretation of Catholicism, which differed radically from Vatican theology.[14]

For Vivien, death has the additional attraction of bringing the happiness that life forbids, for the mistress moves forever out of arm's reach, and to capture her would be to destroy her prized virginity. It is safer to lose the beloved than to win her love. Faced with this dilemma, the narrator of *A Woman Appeared to Me* writes an agonizing letter to San Giovanni during her pilgrimage to Spain, in which she proclaims, *"All is over between us [Vally and me]: It's the best reason for me to continue to adore her."*[15] Death remains the sole solution to this paradox. The narrator explains: *"I dream of a voluptuous death, of a death that would be a consolation for having lived. And this death would be the Impossible Happiness that one has never caught a glimpse of. My obsession with death is like a desire that is excited by a beloved woman."*[16] But whereas for the Metaphysical poets, say, death and sexuality could be wittily confused, for Vivien's characters the identification is a literal, and fatal, one.

Death, sex, and mystical transport are also inextricably entwined in Vivien's poetry because all three hold the promise of transcendence. Increasingly, death becomes the most important component of her religion of love because the transcendence offered is permanent and perfect, while it still retains certain of the thrills of sexuality. As previously noted, according to Susan Gubar, Vivien's cult of death has certain, if limited, positive literary value. Vivien "subversively implies . . . that the lesbian is the epitome of the decadent and that decadence is fundamentally a lesbian literary tradition."[17] Thus, Vivien initially borrows but then recreates and reclaims decadence for herself.

Though it might seem more convenient to trace Vivien's cult of death to the anoxeria of her last years, this preference for death over all else is evident in 1901 in Renée Vivien's first volume of poetry, *Etudes and Preludes*. In a poem "Amazone" ("Amazon"), the warrior woman of the title chooses death even over the most tender caress:

> Elle exulte, amoureuse étrange de la mort. . . .
>
> Son désir, défaillant sur quelque bouche blême
> Dont il sait arracher le baiser sans retour,
> Se penche avec ardeur sur le spasme suprême,
> Plus terrible et plus beau que le spasme
>   d'amour.
>
> She exults, strange lover of death. . . .
>
> Her desire, fainting over some pale mouth
> From which she knows how to tear an
>   unrequited kiss,
> Fervently turns her attention to the
>   supreme spasm,
> More terrible and more beautiful than
>   love's spasm.[18]

But throughout her poetry Vivien is uncertain about what lies beyond this moment of ultimate orgasm. Like Baudelaire, she reels between ecstasy and nothingness. Most commonly, she imagines a serene emptiness, a memory made blank by the waters of Lethe, a place where "I am going to bury my dead: / My dreams, my desires, my grief, my remorse."[19] And this sentiment expressed in 1902 seems quite compatible with one expressed at the end of her life in "Regard en arrière" ("Looking Back"), where Vivien describes death as a state in which she "can sleep / My voyage completed, / In the deep security of oblivion."[20] In this mood, Vivien can only view an afterlife complete with consciousness and memory as a punishment. In "La Légende de Saule" ("The Legend of Saul"), she describes the sorrow of a Hamadryad cursed with eternal life and perpetual memory: "But, possessing immortal life like all other Divinities of imperishable Hellas, she [the Hamadryad] cannot forget her grief. . . . She is the Afflicted One, she is the Inconsolable One, and she weeps long green tears eternally into the rivers."[21] Faced with the prospect of eternal mourning, Vivien prefers oblivion: ". . . I no longer wish for anything except oblivion."[22] Yet on certain occasions, she may express a belief in immortality, especially in the form of reincarnation. As we have seen, there is some discussion about reincarnation in *A Woman Appeared to Me*. In one posthumously published poem, which may have been edited to reinforce the notion that Vivien converted from paganism to Catholicism when she was dying, she expresses some hope that she will be resurrected: "Let someone come to save me / From the twilight where terror is trapped . . . Help! . . ."[23] It is noteworthy that even here the saving figure is female.

It should be pointed out that even though Vivien desired to forget, she did not want to be forgotten. She alternated between the hope that beautiful young women of the future would remember her and the fear that she would be utterly forgotten. She returned frequently to that line of Sappho's which called to her across the millennia and which she translated as: "Someone, I believe, will remember us in the future."[24] But she also suspected that "I will die out, without flowers, without laurel leaves, without hope. . . ."[25] Perhaps one of the attractions of an early death was the Romantic hope that it would ensure her permanent fame.

Although Barney also showed some interest in the transformation of Christian emblems into a religion of love, this particular concatenation of death, sex, and ecstasy was not a blend which had much attraction for her. She, too, was enamored with the figure of the decadent Virgin and once paid tribute in an early sonnet to a maiden whose ". . . breasts are two large wilted flowers, / Cradling their poison with milking desire / Like lotuses on a stagnant swamp."[26] Here, the purity of the Virgin has been contaminated by references to poison and stagnant swamps. The Virgin laughs, but joylessly. While Barney's Virgin is almost as permeated with images borrowed from the Decadent movement as is the pest-ridden Madonna created by Vivien, Barney did not believe that death was a

natural or essential component of her religion of love. She worshipped life
with the same intensity as Vivien adored death. Barney's marginal note to
Vivien's poem entitled, "Let the Dead Bury Their Dead," was an acerbic,
"But not the Living."[27] Nevertheless, it is important to note that in a
sonnet written on the occasion of Vivien's death, Barney appears substan-
tially to respect and accept Vivien's point of view: "How desirable your
early death seems to me! / To survive to a ripe old age, and to die
venerable / Bourgeois like Hugo—or even like Chenier, / Full of pride, to
the hangman she delivers her young head. . . ."[28]

Closely associated with Catholic imagery as a source for inspiration
was the courtly love tradition. It provided Vivien's and Barney's creations
with a literary tradition in which the female figure was a central object of
worship and with a series of costumes, postures and attitudes which
satisfied their demand that theory be made actual whenever possible. It
was almost inevitable that Barney and Vivien should turn to the tradition
of courtly love as a model, for it occupied the same ground that they were
attempting to stake out for women: a territory where the distinction
between the sacred and the profane disappears in a deliberate confusion of
the physical world with the realm of transcendent spirituality. Moreover,
the courtly love tradition wholly overturned the ordinary sexual hier-
archy operating in the real world—the lady may be, indeed, is required to
be, as fully autocratic, demanding, and unreasonable as any lord or husband.

Furthermore, courtly love was an expression of the theory and practice
of relationships which could exist only among a tiny minority at the very
top of society—that is, at court. This exclusivity and elitism were congenial to Barney in particular who never for one moment imagined herself
as the center of a mass movement. In theory, courtly love represented a
revolution in the conceptualization of women; in practice, it was a palace
revolution, though one which would ultimately, over the centuries, affect
heterosexual relationships, ironically helping to create the very foundations of the late nineteenth-century bourgeois marriage which Barney
and Vivien so detested.

Ironies aside, what both writers found provocative in the conventions
of courtly love was the centrality of the beloved women and the role
reversal which the tradition entailed. Nor were they over-interpreting the
evidence. As C. S. Lewis points out, the change is notable even within the
work of a single author, Chrétien de Troyes. In his early *Erec*, Enide is

barely consulted as she is betrothed to Erec. She is required to groom his horse and, later in the poem, to hold it all night while Erec sleeps peacefully, snugly wrapped in her cloak.[29] All these violations of courtesy would be inconceivable in Chrétien's other great chivalric romances, *Launcelot*—or *Tristan*, for that matter—where the key situation is the utter, and even reasonless, humiliation of the lover at the arbitrary whim of Queen Guinevere.

Although neither Barney nor Vivien directly acknowledged the influence of the poetry of Languedoc on her conception of the religion of love, the influence is unmistakable. "Love is the only religion,"[30] one of Barney's characters declares in an unfinished play, "The Mystery of Psyche." Virtually the same phrase was used by her friend and mentor, Remy de Gourmont, who added, in a letter to her, that love was the only religion "which can please a delicate being."[31] Renée Vivien likewise echoed this sentiment through her poetic counterpart, San Giovanni, in *A Woman Appeared to Me:* "I have glorified the love of noble harmony and of feminine beauty to the level of Faith. Any belief which inspires ardor and sacrifice is a true religion."[32]

In the courtly romances, the mistress' power over the lover was absolute—she ruled his thoughts, disturbed his sleep, directed his deeds. The female objects of Barney's and Vivien's devotion and desire were similarly powerful. They identified with the pages/suitors, on their knees, supplicant and yearning before the women who, ideally, remained forever slightly out of reach. As in the courtly romances, the posture is a fixed one, and the appropriate attitude is one of devotion, humiliation, and unquestioning subservience. In her epigrams, Barney once inquired: "Is there any religious order which is stricter? What are hairshirts, forced vigils and fasts, compared to involuntary insomnia, torments, doubts, cruelty, and obsessions, all of which are created by love?"[33] Vivien agreed that love was the highest religion, but for her, too, it was a belief which irrevocably included a Christian conception of pain and suffering as integral components of adoration. The preface to Vivien's first book, *Etudes and Preludes*, is a strongly worded poetic dedication to the ideal woman:

> *Je tremblais. De longs lys religieux et blêmes*
> *Se mouraient dans tes mains, comme des cierges*
> > *froids.*
> *Leurs parfums expirants s'échappaient de tes*
> > *doigts*

En le souffle pâmé des angoisses suprêmes.
De tes clairs vêtements s'exhalaient tour à
                                                    tour
L'agonie et l'amour.

I trembled. Long religious, pale lilies
Died in your hands, like cold candles.
Their dying fragrance escaped from your
                                        fingers
In the swooning breath of supreme anguish.
From your light clothes exuded one by one
        Agony and love.[34]

The strength of Vivien's images here is underscored by her choice of italic type for the poem. What is truly remarkable about this poem is less its use of religious symbolism than the degree to which these symbols are transfused with a kind of tremulous sensuality which owes as much to Baudelairean synesthesia as it does to courtly love. It should be pointed out as well that this poem may be found in Vivien's first collection of verse, which again indicates that her recourse to Christian imagery and symbolism predates any suggested religious conversion. They seem more directly traceable to a literary tradition than to a particular religious experience.

It is tempting to attribute the characteristic celebration of suffering which these lines express to some psychological quirk or peculiarity in Vivien's sensibility. Although we cannot discount the personal and particular attraction such a poetic stance had for her, it is nevertheless true that she repeats here a longstanding literary convention which goes back to the later troubadours and which was maintained for at least six hundred years. Although the original impulse of the Provençal poets may have been to celebrate physical love for its own sake,[35] the conflict between this affirming attitude and the developing Christian sexual ethic rapidly produced a shift in emphasis from the joys of fulfillment to the ecstasy of frustration, a shift which has marked Romantic poetry ever since. There is, therefore, nothing especially unique nor particularly neurotic in Barney's or Vivien's choice of role—the throbbing suppliant at the shrine of an unattainable beloved. Like the knight in Chrétien de Troyes, they found their greatest pleasure in renunciation.

In fact, Vivien alleges that the suffering in her quest for the elusive virgin is superior to the joy of fulfillment, and her Symbolist predecessors would have concurred. In *A Woman Appeared to Me,* the narrator announces that Vally represents the suffering that makes happiness contemptible.[36] Later in the novel, the narrator tells Ione: "My soul is so divinely unhappy that I do not wish to console myself for anything in the world."[37] According to this order of value, pain is more compelling than pleasure and certainly more dependable.

Like the knight or page of the courtly romance (for both Barney and Vivien repeatedly confused the two figures), the suitor is completely obedient to every whim of her mistress, no matter how arbitrary or unreasonable, no matter how much pain she causes. In a passage written for *Sapphic Idyll*, Barney dramatizes this relationship:

Flossie: "I ask you only to let yourself be loved . . . adored . . . marveled at. Nothing other than for you, my Nhinon, to let me be your page. . . , your fervent, little loving page."

Nhinon: "I will let you be my page, slave, and servant to my beauty. . . ."

Flossie: "I abdicate all individuality in this blessed hour; I am nothing except your page."[38]

Barney collaborated with Liane de Pougy on this scene before she had met Renée Vivien, whom she might have influenced, for Vivien expressed the same view in "La Maison du passé" ("The House of the Past"), published a year before her death: "They recognize only your order, your law. / Let no one contradict it or transgress it, / My master and my mistress!"[39] Here, as in *A Woman Appeared to Me*, the beloved is an androgynous virgin whose whims are like those of the gods, to be obeyed without question and endured with love and resignation.[40] This theme is frequently repeated in Vivien's novel and in her verse, appearing for the last time in a posthumously published poem, "Pour le lys" ("For the Lily"): "Oh, Woman whom I love! O irreproachable Lily! / So dear that you can only be approached on one's knees. / Shine your very gentle eyes and your gentler face on me."[41] What is sought is the ecstasy of total self-abandonment, of absolute abdication of all responsibility and will. But one suspects that, for Barney, at least, the role of the page was appealing for its dramatic possibilities rather than for its promise of a quasi-religious transcendence. Barney, with her insistence that ideas must be lived, not merely written about, occasionally donned the outfit of a page while pursuing a beloved woman. For instance, she disguised herself as a page to woo Liane de Pougy. On another occasion she dressed as a sailor so that she and Liane would be left alone on a moonlit excursion.[42] She felt, however, that such costumes had their limitations and chided Evalina Palmer for habitually donning ancient Greek togas. She disdained the Marquise de Belboeuf ("Missy"), Colette's reputed lover, because Missy not only wore men's suits in public but also smoked cigars. For Barney, such costumes were clearly connected with romantic escapades or backyard theatricals. There are also several photos of Vivien wearing a page's costume. In two of these, Barney is attired as a virginal damsel. It seems apparent that their relationship must have suffered from their mutual preoccupation with the role of page since both liked to enact the rejected supplicant while neither felt it was her calling to play the role of the virgin!

The modern reader may be tempted to dismiss the religion of love of Barney and Vivien as merely *fin-de-siècle* theatricality; to do so would be to miss the genuinely radical impulse which inspired it. Both writers consistently sought to reclaim for women the whole of Western literary tradition from Sappho to the Symbolists. Their stance was confident and even aggressive, never defensive. What they did not comprehend, though contemporaries like Woolf did, was that this tradition consisted of more than symbols, images, and props: it was informed with the power relationships which had given rise to it. In adopting the imagery of the past to describe love between women, Barney and Vivien were ineluctably led into maintaining the postures of dominance and submission which underlay that language. They could not perceive that such power relationships are inherently pernicious, even when played between women of equal power—or lack of it—within the context of the dominant culture. Like Woolf, Barney and Vivien saw chastity as a valid choice for women, but unlike Woolf, as Jane Marcus has demonstrated, they were unable to transform a "male repressive ideology into a feminist ideology of power."[43]

Nevertheless, by appropriating the language of romance for their own purposes, both writers did succeed in shifting the terms of reference to include love between women and, consequently, to extend the imaginative possibilities inherent in a kind of androgynous role-reversal. Such reversals of role were, to a small degree, already inherent in the language of courtly love: A term of address used by the lover to his mistress was *midons*, which could as appropriately designate a feudal lord.[44] Nor was the poetry of courtly love always addressed by men to women: Beatrice, countess of Die, was one of a number of Provençal women poets who wrote directly of her love for a man.[45] Yet, the poetry of courtly love in France was founded on the twin principles of heterosexuality and adultery. By adopting it to describe relationships between women, Barney and Vivien transformed it.

In the social circumstances which gave rise to Provençal courtly love, the knight remained forever suppliant—he might enjoy his lady's favors, but he could never marry her, according to the conventions of their relationship. Thus, he could never exercise temporal power over her. Yet in Barney's and Vivien's separate but concurring versions of the romance, the roles always remained potentially reversible, in part because the lovers were not confined by social considerations and because both were women. In her final volume of epigrams, Barney notes, "I first endure everything I inflict. Isn't that what they call an equal relationship?"[46] More seriously, Vivien introduces a scene into *A Woman Appeared to Me* in which the female narrator, who has diligently played the suitor to the indifferent Vally and who has taken almost every sort of abuse from her, suddenly turns on the young and innocent Dagmar and seeks to make her suffer:

> At this moment I felt in me the primitive joy of ape-like and cruel little boys, who amuse themselves by wounding and terrifying a wild dove. I would have liked to make this rosy apriline face turn pale, just for the fierce joy of seeing the living intensity of an irresistible emotion in her eyes. What difference did it make, whether I made this indifferent being quiver with terror or love?[47]

Yet, despite the joy of the sensation of power, the androgynous narrator soon abandons Dagmar to return to Vally's service. Even though the role reversal is theoretically possible because of the sameness of gender, the narrator cannot sustain it, for in reality she is the page/suitor.

Vivien also explored the possibility of role reversal in "La Douve" ("The Moat"), published slightly before *A Woman Appeared to Me*. In this version, it is the knight who torments the lady by locking her in a tower and by cruelly ignoring her feelings:

> Que m'importe ton regard triste,
>   Moiré, tel un pigeon?
> Qu'importe à mon trouble égoïste
>   Le rosier sans bourgeon?
> Je suis aussi lâche qu'un homme,
> Et je t'ordonne et je te somme
> De languir en mes baisers comme
>   En un étroit donjon.
>
> What does your sad look matter to me,
>   Watering like a pigeon?

> What does the budless rosebush matter
>   To my egotistical distress?
> I am as cowardly as a man,
> And I order and enjoin you
> To languish in my kisses as
>   In a narrow dungeon.[48]

By stating that she is "as cowardly as a man," the narrator of this poem (the knight) implies that she is, in fact, not a man; however, she can assume the role of the cruel, egotistical, unthinking lover—the position usually reserved by Vivien for the mistress. It is interesting to note that this is Vivien's only poem in which she introduces a lexicon truly associated with courtly love. The poem is filled with terms such as *moat, vassal, tower, incloister, feudal, dungeon, sovereign,* all of which serve to evoke an early medieval setting. As we shall see in the following chapter, Barney and Vivien used the model of the virgin and page as the cornerstone for their concept of gynandry and expanded the fertile tradition of chivalry to include Lesbian love.

Unfortunately, their idealization of the figure of the Virgin/lady had the effect of sexually objectifying her even further than she was already. As an object, only her beauty and what it symbolizes count, so that she becomes further and further removed from a complex and living reality. It is little wonder that Barney and Vivien chose for themselves the role of page and suitor, for while it offered little in the way of direct satisfaction, at least it implied the possibility of choice and change.

For the moment, it is important to note that though Barney often influenced Renée Vivien, in the case of the religion of love Vivien might have been the leading influence in drawing Barney toward a greater spiritual awareness than she might otherwise have achieved. The degree to which Barney was able to absorb Vivien's preoccupation is strikingly evident in a poem which Barney includes in a set of sonnets commemorating Vivien's death. The poem, "Lamentations des Sirènes" ("Lamentations of the Sirens"), which begins with an epigraph from Vivien herself, is a summary in verse of Vivien's prose piece "Psappha charme les Sirènes" ("Sappho Enchants the Sirens"), from *The Woman of the Wolf.* In this poem, however, Vivien appears as a Sappho-like figure, capable of transforming those left behind in a beautiful, mysterious, and magical way: "Our bodies unfurl under a loving wave / And take a pearly hue from breaking day. / We have not even endured long grey evenings, / But we have understood what they have not. . . .[49]

Left to herself, Barney might have been content to dismiss the in-

comprehensible as merely irrelevant, and without Barney's firm ground-
ing in ordinary reality, Vivien might have allowed her thirst for the
ineffable to draw her even further than it did into a mystical and hermetic
isolation. But united by their mutual determination to reclaim for women
the whole of literary and mythic tradition, they each found in the other a
complementary strength which permitted them both to imagine new
literary syntheses which singly neither was probably capable of achiev-
ing.

VI

PARADIGM FOR A NEW SEXUALITY

*modifies
→ the subject*

(In an additional development of their religion of love, both Barney and
Vivien seized upon the elaborate code of knightly behavior, which involved devotion, courtesy, humility, and seduction by means of "fair
words and music and flawless manners and dress,"[1] and stylized it even
further. The knight becomes even more perfect, and ever more perfectable
because she is, in fact, a woman. Perhaps like Joan of Arc, and certainly
like Shakespeare's Rosalind, her masculine attire permits her to pursue
adventure while her underlying female nature allows her to maintain a
level of *gentilesse* impossible to a male knight by reason of his very
gender. Thus Rosalind succeeds in winning Celia's love because she is
gentler and fairer spoken than a genuine man. Barney commented on the
courtly possibilities presented by the Rosalind type in a poem entitled
"Double Being":

> Like a Shakespearean boy of fairy bred—
> A sex perplexed into attractive seeming
> —Both sexes at best, the strangeness so redeeming!—
>
> . . . .
>
> A page-clothed Rosalind to play a part
> A brow of genius and a lonely heart.[2]

The character of the perfect page is found in Vivien's 1904 tale, "Le
Prince charmant" ("Prince Charming"), a fable in which Vivien combines
elements of the courtly romance with the closely allied fairy tale to
produce a tribute to the Lesbian religion of love. The story is founded on
the androgynous possibilities presented by the woman-dressed-as-a-man
and on the ambiguities of the brother/sister relationship also represented
by Rosalind and her twin. Here we have three characters—Sarolta, the
pure and gentle object of desire, and a brother and sister, Bela and Terka,

96

who reverse the usual sexual roles: Bela is frail and tender, Terka, rough and wild. Sarolta loves Bela and has pined for him for years after their separation in youth. She dislikes his sister intensely. When Bela finally returns, he has become the epitome of the courtly page and charming prince. He is notably superior to all other young men, to such a degree that even Sarolta finds it cause for wonder: " 'Why,' Sarolta would ask her fiancé, 'are you worthier of being loved than other young men? Why do you have gentle ways that they do not? Where did you learn the divine words that they never say?' "[3] This is not merely the idle flattery of a woman in love. After the wedding, we discover the real source of her husband's superiority to all other men: He is, in fact, a woman, Terka, masquerading as her brother. The perfection of the manner of the suitor devoted heart and soul to the religion of love could be achieved only by a woman, and not any woman, at that, but one who had quested for and achieved a high degree of gynandry, a character transcending the conventional limitations of "masculine" and "feminine" by combining the most desirable characteristics of both.

The fairy-tale aspects of "Prince Charming" are evident. The sudden revelation at the end, the magical transformation of a figure from man to woman, the fact that Terka and Sarolta live "happily ever after" in Venice or Florence are all elements commonly found in the fairy tale. Yet, the story lacks the unambiguous celebration of heterosexual marriage which is the usual conclusion of such tales, nor is it aimed at an audience of children. Like the fairy tales of Oscar Wilde, to which this story certainly owes a debt, only a sophisticated adult can fully appreciate the complexities suggested by its ending.[4]

If, from a certain point of view, the fairy tale represents a way of accommodating the sexual ethics of the *chansons de geste* to an audience rather less exalted than that of the courts of Provence, "Prince Charming" similarly accommodates the exclusively heterosexual values of the romances to the demands of a rarefied vision of Lesbian sensibility. It is not to reassure the heterosexual reader that we are invited to regard the lovers as forming "a vision of ideal tenderness, lovingly and chastely intertwined,"[5] but to invoke the prospect of the highest form of relationship possible between lovers. The chastity here is not the defensive chastity of certain of the heroines of other stories in this collection, who must fend off the unwanted and unsought attentions of men whose egos inspire their advances. Rather, it is the necessary condition which permits the protagonists to achieve pure androgyny and perfect love. Without chastity, they would lose their standing as knights in the service of the religion of love and descend to the level of those who are slaves of physical necessity.

Natalie Barney tended to confine her working-out of the virgin/page idea to the *tableaux vivants* and amateur theatricals she performed in the garden behind her house on the rue Jacob. Nevertheless, traces of this courtly relationship may be found in her poetry as well. In a sonnet addressed to "La Belle aux désirs dormants" ("The Beauty with Sleeping Desires"), she says: "I would like to sing of your virginal beauty. / Create for you an otherworldly cult, / Surround you with lilies, incense, and candles."[6] She promises not to allow her "carnal rimes" to wound her beloved's

> . . . âme d'opale
> Par l'opacité de leurs ardeurs mâles,
> Je voudrais t'aimer sans briser tes ailes . . .
>
> Je serais vestale et ta candeur blonde
> Ne subirait pas les lèvres troublantes
> Des amants, ni des princesses charmantes.
>
> . . . opal soul
> Through the audacity of my male ardor,
> I would like to love you without breaking
> your wings . . .
>
> I would be your vestal virgin, and your
> blond innocence
> Will not be subjected to the disturbing lips
> Of lovers, or of the princesses charming.[7]

As in Vivien's "Prince Charming," the idealized love relationship here involves the separation of the beloved from the ordinary world and the establishment of a sensual association which does not involve actual physical contact. In a way more characteristic of Vivien than Barney, the poem seems to associate pressing sexual desire with the "male" and to exalt a delicate and carefully preserved virginity as a necessary condition for a perfect union.

The choice of the fairy-tale mode to convey her vision of the higher Lesbian sensibility was particularly adroit on Vivien's part, for it permitted an affirmation of Lesbian sexuality difficult to achieve convincingly within the confines of the realistic fiction of her day. The conventional ending of the fairy tale, in which prince and princess live happily ever after, for example, is a resolution otherwise not permitted to homosexual lovers, who more commonly were condemned to suffering, pain, and death as a penalty for their unorthodox amour. By locating her lovers in the magic world of the fairy tale, Vivien can avoid the conventional sacrifices found at the end of Lesbian fiction in the early decades of this century: Stephen's renunciation of her lover to permit her to pursue a "better" (that is, heterosexual) life in Radclyffe Hall's *The Well of Loneliness*, for example, or the convenient obliteration of the Lesbian character beneath a descending oak in D. H. Lawrence's *The Fox*. The androgynous, chivalrous prince also eliminates the difficulty of explaining the characters in then-current psychological terminology, as Hall did in her novel.

Nevertheless, "Prince Charming" takes place in a real country (Hungary) and is told as a first-person narrative by a mother to her daughter. Although Hungary is exotically remote, it is not the Forest of Arden, and thus the reader is invited to imagine that Terka and Sarolta were real and, by implication, that their success could, with luck, be duplicated anywhere in Europe. Thus, the heterosexual reader may, if she chooses, view the tale as a slightly outré divertissement, but for the Lesbian, it could become the material for dreams.

Barney and Vivien were working in a milieu in which androgyny was a popular literary topic. The turn of the century marked the rediscovery of some ancient Greek literature, including a number of Sappho's fragments. In addition, the Symbolists had stimulated a renewed interest in the literature of ancient Greece, which included Plato's famous myth of the androgyne. When the androgynous ideal is discussed, most typically the being which emerges is imagined as predominantly male, softened, made more emotive or more creative by the repossession of the suppressed female self.[8] Commonly, for example, when citations are made to Plato's *Symposium*, what is stressed is the heterosexual nature of the first, complete beings; forgotten is Plato's idea that these beings came in three types—all male, all female, and mixed.[9] Even as contemporary a commentator as Mircea Eliade refers to the androgyne as the "perfect man, that is to say a 'complete being.' "[10] Thus, the androgynes of Barney and Vivien are unique in that they begin with the Platonic model but always place the female principle in the primary position.

Although there are many models for the androgyne in literature and although some historians of religion, such as Mircea Eliade, have been able to trace the model back to ancient India as well as to the Biblical account of the separation of Adam and Eve into two beings,[11] the model that Barney in particular refers to is Séraphita-Séraphitus from Balzac's *Séraphita*. While Balzac's novel is "patently based on Swedenborg's doctrine, for the novel was primarily written to illustrate and comment on the Swedenborgian theories of the perfect man,"[12] there is no evidence to suggest that Barney or Vivien ever read Swedenborg directly. In her *pensées*, however, Barney described the protagonist of Balzac's novel as

> . . . Séraphita-Séraphitus—a being complete in her duality—seduces both members, but doesn't wish to form half of a couple.
> Séraphita-Séraphitus, having disturbed both the young woman and her fiancé, leaves them to one another to partake of some metaphysical heaven of which she bears the secret. She animates terrestrial love and surpasses it to become an angel again—such is the double being she is.[13]

While seemingly unaware of the source of this higher being who leaves behind delights of terrestrial love for the higher plane of existence, she does recognize the Swedenborgian concept of perfection and completeness.

In this persistent notion of the formation of the gynandrous whole, which emerges with a predominantly female character, the influence of Barney on Vivien is particularly seen. Although neither woman systematized her thinking on this question, both attempted on several occasions to work out the implications of their theory of androgyny in their poetry and prose. The aim of the creation of the gynandromorph is the emergence of a higher, more perfect being, which would re-establish the principle of Femaleness in the universe. Perhaps prodded by her reading of Nietzsche, or merely by the contemporary fascination with the implications of social Darwinism, Barney was prompted to write in her *pensées* that "a superman can only be born from the purity of a conscious and free woman."[14] Thus, Barney insisted on the emergence of a new, free woman as a prior condition to human advance, and she reversed the values of Nietzsche, who seemed determined to obliterate all feminine values, except in accepting women as passive vessels in the procreation of the Superman.[15]

Aspects of the emerging androgyne can be found in a number of places in the works of both Barney and Vivien. One type is the androgyne who seeks completion in an opposite being—a wholly complementary being containing totally opposite characteristics to the original. For Vivien, Hamlet and Ophelia are certainly a model for this sort of gynandromorph in process. As Vivien declared in a 1903 sonnet about an unnamed woman:

Tu mêles la discorde et le désir aux pleurs,
Grave comme Hamlet, pâle comme Ophélie.

Tu passes, dans l'eclair d'une belle folie,
Comme Elle, prodiguant les chansons et les
                                        fleurs,
Comme Lui, sous l'orgueil dérobant tes
                                douleurs,
Sans que la fixité de ton regard oublie.

Souris, amante blonde, ou rêve, sombre amant.
Ton être double attire ainsi qu'un double
                                        aimant,
Et ta chair brûle avec l'ardeur froide d'un
                                        cierge.

Mon cœur déconcerté se trouble quand je vois
Ton front pensif de prince et tes yeux bleus de
                                        vierge,
Tantôt l'Un, tantôt l'Autre, et les Deux à la
                                        fois.

Grave like Hamlet, pale like Ophelia,
You blend discord and desire with tears.

Like Her, you pass by, in a flash
Of beautiful madness, gushing forth songs and
                                        flowers,
Like Him, under the concealed pride of your
                                grief,
With the determined look never forgetting.

Smile, blond woman lover, or dream, somber
                                male lover.
Your double being draws like a loving double,
And your flesh burns with the cold ardor of a
                                candle.

My disconcerted heart is flustered when I see
Your pensive prince's brow and your blue
                                virgin's eyes,
Sometimes One, sometimes the Other, and Both at
                                once.[16]

Like Terka-Bela, the brother-sister androgyne in "Prince Charming," the emergent gynandrous being in this poem is unarguably female, though retaining qualities which are identifiably masculine, largely through their association with the male Hamlet. The male character-type which lends himself best to gynandrous combinations for Vivien is virginal, as is, of course, the female character.

This type of gynandromorph appears frequently in Barney's plays. Her unpublished "Salle des pas perdus" ("Room of the Lost")—which in some ways curiously anticipates Sartre's *No Exit*—has as its theme the creation of this new being. After death, the characters find themselves in a kind of waiting room where they hope to find their complements so that, at midnight, they may move to a higher plane of existence. The characters are generalized, unspecific types, identified by their social roles, such as Grandmother or Soldier, or even more simply, as She or He. They are not even graced with specific physical identities: She and He, for example, "have no particular facial expressions: They are two masks of youth."[17] Everyone except the soldier finds a match: The old gentleman finds a married woman; She and He, a young couple killed in an auto accident, are reunited; a young girl who has committed suicide is reunited with her grandmother; another woman finds the baby she has yearned for. Clearly, wholeness may be achieved in a number of combinations.

Barney's fullest treatment of the concept of gynandry appears in her self-published novel, *The One Who Is Legion, Or A.D.'s After-Life*. The genderless narrator begins as a shadow in a graveyard, which she/he is able to leave by merging with the One, at which point Stella, the Glow-Woman, reanimates the pair, but they are reborn without memory. The new being wanders to a chapel where she/he finds a book entitled "The Love Lives of A.D." Although never directly stated, it seems evident that A.D. and the narrator are the same. The book contains love letters to A.D. from both male and female admirers; the bookends in the chapel are made of breasts. The implication is that A.D., whose gender is unspecified, was bi- or perhaps pan-sexual, though the breasts suggest that A.D.'s particular interest was in women. Ironically, A.D.'s adventures beyond traditional moral convention did not free her/him. On the contrary, A.D. became completely enslaved by the physical side of the self and finally committed suicide. It is A.D.'s new self, the narrator, who, by putting aside carnal love, becomes gynandrous. In this new state the narrator is at once everyone and no one—that is, legion. She/he is able to enter into the emotions and imaginations of others, unbound by the particular limitations of sexuality, gender, or even personality. Barney here seems to be echoing the Jungian notion of the androgynous component of creativity, a point that she was to make explicit in a later essay in *Traits and Portraits*: "And if he [man] . . . experiences some inclination towards the arts, doesn't he owe it to the muses who presided at his birth and who have dedicated him so that he could become this hybrid—the artist?"[18]

If artists are hybrids, the fully-evolved gynandromorph is a hermaphrodite—there is "no marrying in heaven."[19] Indeed, one of the attractions of the movement toward this higher self-sufficient state in *The One Who Is Legion* is that one is relieved of the burden of carnal sexuality, of the "sad repetition of conjugal and other loves—far less diverting with its thirty-two positions (who has retained interest enough in the sex game to try each of them?) . . . exercises in which, after a few little shrieks, one is deposited at the entrance much as before starting."[20] The price of living "infinitely may be to love infinitely little,"[21] but the jaded tone of this novel suggests that Barney felt that this release was probably all to the good, and obviously a necessary condition for attaining gynandry.

Asexuality also characterizes San Giovanni in Vivien's *A Woman Appeared to Me,* but her version of the gynandromorph is more evidently female than A.D., who is strictly neuter. San Giovanni clearly breathes a purer, more rarefied atmosphere than ordinary humankind. Her body exists merely to permit her to produce divine poetry for a world altogether too materialistic and temporal to appreciate it.

Vivien's gynandromorph is sexless and has no need to reproduce, since her angelic qualities imply that she is immortal. Like other Vivien heroines, she is a virgin, untouched and untouchable, but her sexlessness makes her no longer vulnerable to men's lust. For Vivien, the notion of gynandry had the clear advantage of eliminating the one function she granted to men as indispensable—reproduction, the perpetuation of "this crime: life."[22] Although technically asexual, the gynandromorph is not genderless, for San Giovanni represents the triumph of the Female principle over the evil male principle, at least in the eyes of Vally: "Everything that is ugly, unjust, ferocious, and cowardly emanates from the Male Principle. Everything that is painfully beautiful and desirable emanates from the Female Principle."[23] Nevertheless, even at a point at which the female principle appears to have triumphed, at least in Vivien's imagination, the beauty which flows from it is still a mournful beauty, tinged with Symbolist melancholy far more than with feminist optimism.

The intense interest that Barney and Vivien showed in the gynandromorph was shared by other members of Barney's salon. For example, Romaine Brooks provided the drawings for *The One Who Is Legion,* her stylized figures placing women beyond any traditional definition. The affinity of her vision to Barney's and Vivien's clearly emerges in these drawings. The thin, stick-like figures, which look more dead than alive, hang in space in poses suggestive of crucifixion. Indeed, they seem to have paid with their lives to achieve this higher form of being. Perhaps Brooks's drawings suggest that society demands that women give up life itself in return for a different sexuality or that the price for creating a third sex might prove higher than expected.

As a portraitist, Brooks was primarily intrigued with some of the real-life gynandrous women she met in Barney's salon and in Paris in general. Two of her works—"Peter, a Young English Girl," and "Renate Borgatti au piano"—portray women who can only be identified as such by the title of the portrait. Peter, a young, thin woman with extremely short hair is shown in profile. She is dressed in a dark, belted man's jacket, a man's white shirt, tie, and vest. Her right hand relaxedly loops over the belt in a pose many would regard as "masculine." Peter might certainly pass for a handsome, effete dandy.[24] Renate Borgatti is the epitome of the artistic male pianist at work. Dressed in a cape, which seems to cover a suit, Borgatti plays intently at her piano as she gazes at the keys with drooped lids. The hair, which reaches only slightly below her ear, and the strong hands with their long, lean fingers, denote a professional pianist, not a Victorian maiden playing for the entertainment of guests.[25] Brooks might have left the viewer happily confused about the sexual identity of her subjects, but by giving the portraits unmistakable titles, she forces us to confront the ambiguity of her subjects and the nature of our own stereotypes about femininity and masculinity.

Feminists might quickly recall Virginia Woolf's *Orlando*, though technically speaking, Orlando is not an androgyne since she/he alternates between male and female identities without actually combining the two. As Sandra Gilbert put it, Orlando is more a "metaphorical transvestite"[26] than a real androgyne. Though the clothing changes, at heart the person remains the same.

In Paris, the theme was of particular interest to Paule Riversdale, who, as was mentioned earlier, may have been another pseudonym for Renée Vivien. Riversdale deals with androgyny in several of her novels, most extensively in *L'Etre double (Double Being)*, in which she recasts Socrates' myth. Essentially, most androgynous models subsumed the female into the male principle, or at best tried to balance the two.

Riversdale, in contrast, creates a complicated myth of androgyny, consisting of several stages, which have been extensively analyzed by Jeanne Manning in her dissertation on Renée Vivien. The Great Mother, Ishtar, creates the original "perfect being," but because it is unique, "it is forbidden to procreate with inferior beings and is to remain sterile because it could never find its equal."[27] Tormented by its difference, the Hermaphrodite finally chooses death, since "only death will deliver your burdensome body, only death will return you to the infinite."[28]

In the second stage, the Hermaphrodite is reborn. For Riversdale, the creation of the double being is not a gentle, uplifting combination of the two genders. Rather, gynandry results from a tremendous battle in which the male principle, represented by fire, is finally squelched by the female principle, represented by water.[29] Thus, the resulting gynad is primarily female.

"In the final regeneration of the Hermaphrodite into 'l'Etre Parfait,' . . . the distinct and separated elements . . . seek to come together and are born again into a new creation. It represents the fusion of the best qualities of both sexes and the desire for harmonious coexistence of masculine and feminine qualities."[30] The final version seems closest in tone and content to Socrates' original myth.

On the surface the versions may seem a bit contradictory and may in the end appear to revert to a male model. Closer investigation reveals an underlying feminist analysis of androgyny. Riversdale suggests in a radical way that combining male and female principles is not an appropriate solution, for there are evil elements inherent in masculinity. Therefore, the dark side of masculinity must be eradicated before any attempt to unite the sexes can be undertaken.

Other members of Barney's coterie were also intrigued by the concept of androgyny. Lucie Delarue-Mardrus wrote a novel in 1930 entitled *The Angel and the Perverts*, which is purportedly about Natalie Barney. The novel is about a hermaphrodite who leads two lives under two names— Marion Hervin and Mario de Valdeclare. People of both sexes are attracted to this character, but she/he scorns their advances. Like Riversdale's Hermaphrodite, the angel here is superior to others and unable to connect with ordinary human beings. She/he is ultimately neuter.

There seemed to be some agreement among the members of the Paris salon that the fate of the androgyne was an unhappy one, whether because she/he is unable to connect with the rest of society or because others persecute her/him for being different. Colette suggested that happiness was actually antithetical to the state of androgyny. "There especially remains for the androgynous creature the right, even the obligation, never to be happy. If jovial, the androgynous creature is a monster. But it trails irrevocably among us its seraphic suffering, its glimmering tears."[31]

Though the theme of androgyny gained a modicum of popularity in the first decades of the twentieth century, Barney and Vivien were more radical than their peers in developing a paradigm for this new sexuality, one which stressed a vital and often unmentioned (and unmentionable) part of the "third sex," that is, Lesbianism. What is noteworthy about "Prince Charming," for example, as well as about other works by both Barney and Vivien which deal with Lesbianism, is not merely what it includes, but what it omits. All of their works lack any kind of apologia for daring to raise the subject. None of their works contain what had come to be the conventional disclaimer, presumptively written by a psychiatrist or medical authority, which sanitized works ranging from *Diana: A Strange Autobiography* by Diana Frederics to the "Lesbian pulp novels" of the 1950s.[32] Barney and Vivien neither explained nor apologized and yet were never persecuted or prosecuted for their work. Their immunity is the more remarkable in view of the difficulties experienced by others who attempted to create an image of homosexuality in literature which was something other than merely sensational. Radclyffe Hall's book was tried both in England and in the United States and banned in both countries; as late as the 1930s, the authorities in most European countries successfully demanded that the positive ending of Christa Winsloe's *Mädchen in Uniform* be replaced by the obligatory catastrophe.[33] Although a number of Barney's and Vivien's contemporaries— among them writers as eminent as Gertrude Stein, who wrote erotic poetry to Alice B. Toklas, and E. M. Forster, who wrote the homosexual novel *Maurice*—were persuaded by this atmosphere to delay publishing their homoerotic books until after their deaths, Barney and Vivien themselves remained unequivocally open in announcing both their sexual preference and their determination to write about it. Nevertheless, they were unquestionably protected to a degree by their decision to live in Paris and write in French, the language of Proust's *Remembrance of Things Past* and Gide's *Corydon*.

Although Barney and Vivien did depend for protection to a degree on the greater license afforded by French literature to explore homosexual themes and did as well draw on the well-established tradition in Symbolist literature of homoerotic reference, it is interesting to note how much further they were able to go than were their symbolist predecessors. Despite the fact that Baudelaire, for example, at least admitted Lesbians into his poetry, he brought them in only to condemn them, as the title of one of the poems in the series, "Femmes damnées," suggests. Both Verlaine and his lover, Rimbaud, wrote homoerotic poetry, but these can be seen, as indeed they were, as part of a literary stance as *enfants terribles*, not as a serious challenge to the values of the ordinary man, who might indeed feel smugly superior to these reckless poets who risked their health with drugs and sex and, in Rimbaud's case, who died so young. Whereas Vivien did respect the conventions sufficiently to confine her explorations of Lesbian sexuality to fiction and verse, Barney was not so circumspect. In her *pensées* and in her essays, she confronted her heterosexual readers directly, engaging them in the dialectic of sex. By addressing herself to contemporary issues such as reproduction, overpopulation, and the definition of "normality," as well as by summoning up historical precedent, Barney allowed her readers no comforting escapes. Her essay, "L'Amour défendu" ("Forbidden Love"), opened new territory to literary discussion and ranks as one of her significant achievements. As Gayle Rubin has observed, Barney and Vivien "achieved and articulated a distinctively lesbian self-awareness. Their writings show that they understood who they were and what they were up against. There were few homosexuals of either sex who comprehended the dimensions of the homosexual situation."[34]

It is true that Barney and Vivien developed this consciousness on the foundation of the more or less common sense of alienation experienced and articulated by a number of homosexual writers both before and after them. Male and female homosexuals in the nineteenth century, when they were granted literary existence at all, were always excluded from ordinary society, like Balzac's Vautrin or the *femmes damnées* of Baudelaire. In the early twentieth century, more detailed, complex, and "inside" accounts of the lives of Lesbians and gay men began to appear, though these tended still to be encoded, permitting those readers who preferred to ignore their homosexual content to do so. The intricate interrelations, intrigues, and deceptions which Lesbian and gay men employed for their survival were elaborately portrayed by Marcel Proust in *Remembrance of Things Past*. In *The Immoralist*, André Gide explored the complicated existence of men who are attracted to male adolescents.[35] Colette drew a marvelous portrait of the "Ladies of Llangollen" who ran away together and spent fifty-three years in rural Wales.[36]

But the book which attracted the most attention to the subject of Lesbianism and which set the tone for the public debate of the question was Radclyffe Hall's *The Well of Loneliness*. In many ways, *The Well* is the epitome of a pattern of Lesbianism in the English novel, which "made homosexuality perverse," as Catharine Stimpson puts it, for *The Well* includes "the dying fall, a narrative of damnation, of the lesbian's suffering as a lonely outcast attracted to a psychological lower caste."[37] The protagonist, Stephen Gordon, views her homosexuality as a species of congenital deformity. She believes her difference condemns her to

> loneliness, or worse still, far worse because it so deeply degraded the spirit, a life of perpetual subterfuge, of guarded opinions and guarded actions, of lies of omission if not of speech, of becoming an accomplice in the world's injustice by maintaining at all times a judicious silence . . . because if they knew they would turn aside, even the friends one respected.[38]

As Esther Newton points out, Gordon is a " 'mannish lesbian,' . . . a figure who is defined as a lesbian *because* her behavior or dress (and usually both) manifest elements designated as exclusively masculine."[39] In other words, Hall's protagonist is a freak of nature, beyond acceptable definitions of gender.

Though nothing could be further from the attitude of Natalie Barney in particular than this condition of covert despair, she and Renée Vivien did share with Radclyffe Hall and other Lesbian and gay male writers a general sense of being different and the recognition that society despised the difference. Renée Vivien summed up her sense of alienation in one line: "Everywhere I go I repeat: *I do not belong here.*"[40] Vivien had seen people turn from her in disgust, an experience described as well by Hall. She feelingly described the intense hatred of heterosexuals for her kind in several poems, including "Paroles à l'amie" ("Words to a Woman Friend") and "Sans fleurs à votre front . . ." ("Without Flowers on Your Brow"): "They have made irritated gestures at me with their hands / Because my look sought out your tender look . . . / Seeing us pass by, no one wished to understand / That I chose you with simplicity."[41]

Lines such as these indicate precisely where Barney and Vivien differed from virtually every writer on a homosexual theme who had preceded them or, indeed, who were contemporaries. Vivien's response to society's disdain is neither an acknowledgment of guilt nor an expression of shame or anguish. Rather, she affirms that she has made her choice "with simplicity." Stephen Gordon's cry of despair, " 'What am I in God's name—some kind of abomination?' "[42] finds no echo in the work of either Vivien or Barney. Instead they remain unruffled by society's antagonism: Vivien goes on to remind Christ that she has never believed in his strict laws and affirms that she has lived her life as a "simple pagan."

Barney as well was evidently willing to describe her entire existence in terms of her essential nonconformity. Echoing Descartes, she remarked: "They say that it is necessary 'to conform.' I have never conformed; nevertheless, I exist."[43] She considered that Lesbianism conferred on her a "perilous advantage" which presented her with the challenge of living her life courageously.[44] From her point of view, the ordinary heterosexual woman was part of a cowardly herd comprised of those who had neither the courage nor the conviction to hear the call of Sappho's lyre.[45] She felt, like Axël and Sara in Villiers de l'Isle-Adam's *Axël*, that only the lower orders would take any interest in performing the viler tasks of sexuality, like reproduction: "A husband does what he must / Creating tons of children, but that's for the masses!"[46] Elsewhere, in a sonnet, Barney castigates a woman who wished to have a son as "a beast reproducing the evils of your ancestors."[47] She described reproduction as "the vilest of tasks. Gods do not reproduce themselves: They themselves are their own masterpieces."[48] Here the common reproach to homosexuals that their failure to reproduce renders them inferior is neatly countered; rather than a liability, the childlessness of the Lesbian is viewed as a mark of distinction, as a sign that she approaches nearer the gods than the common woman can hope to do, being more perfect.

Both Barney and Vivien evinced considerable disgust at the processes of childbearing. It might be tempting to attribute their response to some psychological peculiarity, but it is hardly necessary to do so, for they had both literary and political support for their position. In the first place, there was of course their inheritance from their Symbolist and Decadent mentors, who were frequently too interested in a minute and loving examination of death to spare much thought to the continuation of the species. Furthermore, human fertility was too closely connected with bourgeois family values to be wholly congenial to the Symbolists. It should, however, be pointed out that the effects of uncontrolled reproduction on the lives of women had led a number of turn-of-the-century feminists to view maternity with considerable suspicion, and often to reject sexuality in terms not unlike those used by Barney and Vivien to describe childbirth. In Charlotte Perkins Gilman's Utopian feminist novel, *Herland*, for example, motherhood is highly valued, but it is a motherhood achieved only once in the lifetime of a woman and achieved asexually as well, through a mystically-described parthenogenic process. The product of this birth is, of course, a replica of the mother, so that, in a sense, the heterosexual Gilman and the Lesbian Barney agree that "the most beautiful life is that in which one creates oneself instead of procreating another."[49]

Furthermore, both Barney and Vivien came from immensely privileged circumstances, from that section of society which could, and did, view maternity as a choice rather than an inevitable fate. It was her failure to comprehend the actual limitations on the choice of the majority of women which caused Barney to lay some of the blame for their oppression on women's own lassitude or laziness. Nevertheless, as was the case for a number of radical suffragists, their antireproductive stance must also be viewed as representing their rebellion against the traditional roles assigned to women in society. If ordinary women must marry and reproduce, then Barney's and Vivien's nonconformity would give them the option to do neither.

The strategy which Barney and Vivien adopted to defend their sexuality was an aggressive one. Rather than pleading for toleration on the grounds that their lives were the product of uncontrollable destiny or congenital abnormality for which they could hardly be held responsible, they went on the offensive, attacking heterosexual institutions as disgusting and abnormal. The implication of this stance is that Lesbianism must be viewed as a style of life competing with heterosexuality, and an equally valid one. Characteristically, they turned the heterosexual attack back on the heterosexuals themselves, using much the same language and many of the same emotions. In Barney's case, this kind of transformation could frequently be extremely witty; for Vivien, it came from the soul.

The typical heroine in a work by Barney or Vivien cherishes her virginity, even at the price of death or exile. To both writers, the consummation of marriage was a vile act of defilement or rape. Vivien often used the pejorative terms *rut* and *filth* to describe heterosexual copulation. Physical connection between the sexes struck her as a kind of gross abnormality. When Vally asks San Giovanni in *A Woman Appeared to Me* if a woman has ever loved a man, San Giovanni replies in disgust: "I can hardly conceive of such a deviation of the senses. Sadism and the rape of little children appear to me infinitely more normal."[50] Vivien's revulsion is underscored by the strength of her comparisons. When confronted with the evidence provided by historical and fictional accounts of great loves, San Giovanni replies that the Juliets and Yseults of literature were in love with love itself, and not with men.[51]

Throughout this partly serious, partly comic novel, Vivien uses the same technique. All of the usual responses to homosexuality, all of the language commonly employed to express righteous disgust at the phenomenon, are here used to describe heterosexual connection. Marriage is seen as "abnormal." Whereas, at the turn of the century, Lesbianism was considered hardly a suitable topic for genteel conversation, in *A Woman Appeared to Me* the announcement of the engagement of a man and a woman is received by San Giovanni with expressions of outraged modesty: "He doesn't fear to offend my modesty by this indecent proclamation of his engagement. There are some improper events that one should avoid mentioning in public."[52] Here the frequently repeated demand by conventional society that homosexuals stop "flaunting" their difference is travestied. San Giovanni's sensitivity is of course absurd, but is it any more ridiculous than the attitude it parodies? On another occasion, San Giovanni vigorously defends a friend accused of heterosexuality: "Sir, that would be a physically impossible aberration. I have too much esteem for our friend to believe her capable of such an abnormal passion."[53] The effect of these reversals is twofold: For the Lesbian reader, they provide the occasion for a delightful revenge for all the contempt and insult suffered at the hands of a smugly self-righteous society convinced of its fundamental normality; for any reader representative of that society hardy enough to read it, the novel provides the opportunity to examine what might have been previously unexamined presumptions from another point of view.

Barney was as opposed to marriage as was Vivien, but she tended to base her attack on wittily intellectual, rather than on emotional, grounds. Nevertheless, she did address an engaged woman in one of her sonnets: "Therefore, you are getting married, immolating your twenty years / As a hostage to the law of ancient wrongs."[54] But in general, she maintained that she couldn't comprehend marriage because it seemed that one was neither alone nor together.[55] When someone suggested to her that marriage was what everyone did as a matter of course and the "natural" thing to do, Barney responded: "The word 'outside of nature' has naturally fallen outside of usage, but let us recognize that nothing could be more against nature than the uniformity that one tries to impose on people."[56] She dismissed uniformity as downright boring.[57]

To Barney, her homosexuality was an integral part of her refusal to conform. She claimed that uniformity only served to create robots, "people without personalities."[58] She believed that the pressure to conform threatened privacy and individuality: "For what does this so-called 'modern world' offer us in exchange for a private life which is becoming more and more menaced? Collective emotions, sustained either by wars with H Bombs, or at least by the 'boxing rings' while we await the bombs."[59] To Barney, the right to an individual existence free of interference was threatened by waves of collective emotions generated by rumors of war or violent spectator sports. Underlying this statement is the implicitly political idea that the pressure to conform sexually is responsible for the increasingly violent tenor of modern existence. As noted earlier, Barney

equated war with the rape of individual women. In addition, she suggested that rape was the model for heterosexual interaction. As Shari
Benstock writes:

> For Barney, lesbian eroticism was defined by a sharing of sensual experi-
> ences, each of the partners taking pleasure in the other's body. This sense of
> equality and sensual exchange distinguished itself from heterosexual prac-
> tice, in which a woman was "taken," "possessed," or "ravished" by the
> male. The heterosexual act made woman a victim of man's desire; lesbian
> sexuality allowed her to direct her own desire and discover through her
> body her own sensual purposes.[60]

Both Barney and Vivien defended homosexuality on a variety of other
grounds. Like any number of other homosexual writers, they looked to
the past for models. As we have seen, Sappho was frequently evoked by
both writers as an irreproachable example of Lesbian genius. Barney also
reminded her readers that the court of Henri III, the sonnets of Shakespeare, and the works of Socrates and Plato reflected homosexual pre-
dilections.[61]

If the past were not justification enough for the essential naturalness of
Lesbianism, modern science also provided support. Barney had read the
works of Havelock Ellis, Krafft-Ebing, Freud, and Jung. She used them to
demonstrate that the real abnormality would be for the Lesbian to try to
become heterosexual. "For the majority of sexually abnormal people, the
abnormality would precisely consist in the practice of a normal sexuality!"[62] Vivien also viewed Lesbianism as biologically normal. In a
poem on the subject, she elaborates on the splendors of female bodies
naturally drawn to one another as the sea is to the moon: "The laughter of
the Moon smitten by the Sea, / The sob of the Sea smitten by the
Moon."[63] Vivien here exploits the feminine gender of the words for *moon*
and *sea* in French to underscore the utter naturalness of the attraction.

To both writers, homosexuality was not only natural but also sanctified
by ancient Greek religion and by the Bible itself. As we have seen, it was
Renée Vivien who was largely responsible for reviving the reputation of
Sappho at the turn of the century as a homoerotic writer. Vivien finds in
Sappho's "Ode to Aphrodite" proof that the goddess approved of love
between women. In Vivien's reinterpretation of Aphrodite's promise to
Sappho that scornful lovers would one day pursue her, the goddess becomes even more assertive in her anger at one who would scorn Lesbian
love: *"I, the daughter of Zeus, will strike down the pride / Of the woman
who flees your embrace, o poet! / You will see her restless shadow /*

Wandering vainly on your doorstep.''[64] Jeanne Manning points out that Vivien consciously recast Sappho's fragments in a Lesbian mode. For example, Vivien expands a single line of Sappho's about the most beautiful stars "into four stanzas that create the ambiance of a Lesbian summer night. Sensuous elements in nature are compatible with the sensibilities of the lovers, and in fact, nature provokes the physical desires which trouble them."[65]

In "Télésilla," Vivien uses Artemis, who fled both males and heterosexual love, as an example of yet another Greek goddess friendly to Lesbianism. A third goddess invoked is the Roman Fauna, who "smiles at the love of intertwined women."[66] Both she and Barney interpreted the Biblical pairs of David and Jonathan and Ruth and Naomi as homosexual. One must observe that in Vivien's meditation on the Book of Ruth, the love between Ruth and Naomi is superior to that between David and Jonathan because it transcends sexuality.[67]

Indeed, it was precisely because both Barney and Vivien believed that Lesbianism represented less a sexual preference than a total commitment to women and the values they represented that they were convinced of the moral basis of their homosexuality. Barney was very careful, in "Forbidden Love," to distinguish Lesbianism from vice—that is, from mere sensual or sexual pleasure devoid of higher emotions: "It is vice where there is neither emotion nor love nor true passion."[68] Lust, in the absence of passionate love capable of transcending self, was clearly wrong to both Barney and to Vivien. "Sensuality founded on inversion cannot become a *raison d'être* in itself, for, if the quest for pleasure is only physically assuaged, everything is lost and even total sensuality might end up as mania."[69]

Barney sought to distinguish Lesbians from male homosexuals, whose promiscuity she found deplorable: "Their erotic exchanges, while ceaselessly preoccupying them, occupy only a moment of their time."[70] Her criticism of detached sensuality, quoted above, is drawn from a discussion of André Gide, whom she characterized as a "Sodomite," that is, one of a class of male homosexuals who sought out their inferiors— younger men—and therefore gained nothing from the connection. She contrasted this behavior with that of Lesbians, whom she termed "Gomorrhean," women who showed "a marked preference for their elders or for their superiors."[71] Obviously, this is Barney's view, but it is interesting that one can turn this on its head and claim that boys are simply doing the same thing! In her use of a Biblical term to refer to the men of whom she did not approve, a term which has been applied pejoratively for centuries to male homosexuals, Barney strongly indicated that she did not feel a common bond with them because she was a Lesbian. Although she defended Gide's right to be different, she deplored "the bad example" that Gide gave to young people "by his promiscuity reduced by erotic needs."[72]

It is not easy to reconcile the rather stern morality of passages like these with what is known of Barney's own enthusiasm for romantic adventure. It was she, after all, who proclaimed that "fidelity is merely the triumph of habit over indiscretion."[73] Her epigrams and other writings would appear to be a testament to promiscuity. She insisted that "forever is too long a time,"[74] and she did not view infidelity as necessarily a fault: "Is it the fault of things or of beings or of ourselves if nothing is able to retain our devotion."[75] Perhaps these observations may most simply be attributed to the *pensée* form itself, which invites a witty and perverse challenge to conventional wisdom. But they may arise as well out of Barney's recognition that she could not hope to discover her ideal of beauty in any one particular woman. As Vally, Barney's counterpart, put it in *A Woman Appeared to Me:*

> The artist who dreams of creating a statue does not seek a single model for his divine vision. He finds absolute splendor through dissimilar beings, each one revealing her most beautiful aspects. As for me, for my impassioned dream, it is necessary to reunite scattered perfections in order to blend them in a harmonious being created by my dreams.[76]

As we have seen, Barney, along with Vivien, forged from the materials of the courtly love tradition a new religion of Lesbian love in which she played the part of the questing knight who sought ideal beauty itself. The true knowledge of beauty and love could be gained only through the self-knowledge attained through experience and adventure.

Herein lies the clue to the difference she drew between herself and the male Don Juan. As Jean Chalon has pointed out, Barney's philosophy demanded that she love and conserve her conquests, whereas the male Don Juan merely runs from victim to victim.[77] Barney maintained that the Don Juan type "aspired only to leave them."[78] She perceived that these sorts of men hated women, that they were often latent homosexuals, and that their acts devolved from mere lust and self-love.[79] Barney, as well as Vivien, condemned mere lust, since the quest for love had to be undertaken in the right spirit of commitment. There had to be a constancy in the infidelity, paradoxical as it may appear.

The reason that Barney could not make a common cause with Gide and those like him was that he fell into the class of those who rarely rise above lust, of those to whom the hunt becomes the end in itself, or so she believed. And so the final defense of homosexuality offered by Barney and Vivien—that it was a way of life, not just a sexual act—necessarily involved a repudiation of those who saw it as something else.

It is precisely here that the significance of the work of Barney and Vivien to contemporary Lesbians and feminists begins to emerge. Beneath the theatricality of their romantic religion of love lay the unshakable conviction that Lesbianism was not merely a defensible alternative to heterosexuality. In its ideal manifestation, it provided the opportunity for a quasi-religious transcendence of the self, and perhaps, at some remove, the transformation of society. In this regard, Barney and Vivien were years ahead of their contemporaries, most of whom, like Radclyffe Hall, found themselves locked in a defensive posture which at best demanded toleration of an inescapable deviance. Their calm confidence is the utter rightness of their Lesbianism is the more remarkable when we consider how relatively recently the idea of homosexuality as a way of life had emerged. It was not until the latter half of the nineteenth century that homosexuals of either gender began to define themselves—and demand that others define them—as such. Previously, homosexuality had been associated with a particular variety of sexual act, not with identifiable cultural behavior.[80] Not only were Barney and Vivien among the first writers to document and celebrate this change in self-awareness in the homosexual community, but they also went so far as to attempt to actualize their dream of a Lesbian culture in their abortive stay on the isle of Lesbos. Furthermore, unlike even Proust's portrayal of a new homosexual society which in the end, for him at least, seems sterile and inferior to the culture of the heterosexual majority, Barney and Vivien believed that Lesbian societies offered positive and viable alternatives to the failures of modern mass culture. Only Colette, in *The Pure and the Impure*, gave so frank and open a glimpse into the Lesbian subculture of Paris, and she was, to a degree, protected by her evident heterosexual proclivities.

Despite these achievements, the claim cannot be made that Barney and Vivien developed a political consciousness resembling that of the Lesbian/feminist movement of the post-Stonewall generation (post-1969). Their transformation of the conventions of courtly love to suit the demands of a Lesbian love-religion sprang from a radical impulse to demonstrate that Lesbianism was at least as worthy as heterosexuality. They could not be expected to anticipate that their uncritical adoption of these conventions locked them into rigid codes of behavior and of sexual ethics.

Their sexual paradigm left a woman with only two choices: to be a virgin, cold and inaccessible, almost indistinguishable from the feminine ideal chiseled in marble by the men who had preceded them, or to be the suitor, kneeling in worship, but lacking that actual temporal power conveyed on real men by patriarchal society.

In contrast, Vivien and, to a somewhat lesser degree, Barney were both innovative in their insistence that the androgynous ideal was identifiably female. Neither, however, was sufficiently free of her Symbolist origins to liberate the concept from specifically nineteenth-century notions of perfection. A. D. and San Giovanni are certainly higher beings, removed from earthly carnality by their "sterile ardor and . . . androgynous charm,"[81] as Vivien put it in one of her early poems, but they are so far removed from temporal possibility that they are all but irrelevant. What worked as the poetic crystalization of an existential attitude for Balzac or Swedenborg is inadequate for Barney and Vivien, whose participation in that attitude was profoundly altered by their recognition of the actual social oppression of women. To a certain degree, therefore, their determination to work within the canon of nineteenth-century aesthetics made it impossible for either writer to construct a viable model of a future relevant to the real concerns of living women. On the other hand, neither Barney nor Vivien ever pretended to be the leader of a Lesbian revolution.

Nevertheless, it must be said in their defense that both Barney and Vivien were determined that inherited myth and symbol could be transformed to work for, rather than against, women. Whether intentionally or not, the nineteenth-century models of the androgyne that they chose to imitate invested masculinity with a dimension of emotional openness of creativity which enhanced the psychic condition of the male without in any way impinging upon his dominance in the world.[82] By inventing the gynandromorph, Barney and Vivien cast the concept of the androgyne into a different light: They proposed a mythic possibility in which the female was retained as an actual principle, not as a secondary sexual characteristic. In this definition, women were allowed to retain their essential identities and to project them forward onto an ideal plane.

VII.

CONCLUSION
FOR THE WOMEN OF THE FUTURE

It is in relationship to each other and to the feminist writers who succeeded them that the true significance of the work of Natalie Barney and
Renée Vivien emerges. The literary connection between the two was
most fruitful, for each woman enlarged the vision of the other. Barney's
acerbic and tough-minded feminism stimulated Vivien to attempt to
embody in fiction examples of the visionary women they both admired.
Vivien's mysticism, while perhaps destructive to herself, acted upon
Barney to deepen and enrich the scope of what might otherwise have
remained a rather facile wit.

In their relationship, Barney was the theoretician and Vivien, the practi-
tioner. In her essays, *pensées*, epigrams, novel, poems, and plays, Barney
articulated the concepts which became the structural elements of Vivien's writing. But Barney devoted far more energy to living her ideas than
to working them out to their fullest theoretical development; therefore,
her most memorable work consists of her "scatterings."

Vivien, on the other hand, never committed a theoretical abstraction,
or if she did, it is locked in the Bibliothèque Nationale until the year
2000, when her papers will be unsealed. But her fundamental agreement
with Barney's rooted feminism may be inferred from the persistence in
her fiction of female characters who are either endowed with traditionally masculine abilities or engaged in male occupations or who, like
Vashti, articulate a position of equality with men for which they are
willing to die.

Barney also affected the circle of women who surrounded her in Paris,
some of whom, at least, are a continuing part of the canon of women's
literature. A number of novelists used Barney as the source for characters
in their own fiction. Colette not only wrote about her friendship with
Vivien in *The Pure and the Impure*, but she also based the character of

117

Flossie in the Claudine series of novels on Barney. As we have seen, Barney also appears in *The Well of Loneliness*, by Radclyffe Hall, as Valérie Seymour. Barney figures unforgettably, and scandalously, as Evangeline Musset in Djuna Barnes's *Ladies Almanack*, in which Evangeline's funeral (decades before Barney's actual death) is the social event of the season. Both Hall and Barnes appear to have admired Barney's liberated attitudes toward life and Lesbian sexuality without being altogether able to share them. Barney appears as well in *The Angel and the Perverts*, a novel by Lucie Delarue-Mardrus, and Barney influenced the Lesbian episodes of Liane de Pougy's *Sapphic Idyll*, which she helped to write. In all these literary manifestations, Barney is consistently unapologetic, unashamed, and guiltless—a sharp contrast to most of the Lesbian characters in the novels written during much of her lifetime.

In her own work as well, Barney boldly refused to encode her Lesbianism in a secret language, as did Djuna Barnes by means of Middle English in her *Ladies Almanack* and Gertrude Stein by means of puns in *Tender Buttons*. Both Barney and Vivien also refused to disguise their feelings as merely "female friendship," though friendship was certainly a significant part of what they felt. Nor did either of them attempt to gain acceptability by pandering to a masculinist view of Lesbianism by creating a voyeuristic thrill for the male reader, as Baudelaire, Balzac, Zola, and others had done before them.[1] Instead of opening a keyhole for men to peer into, they sealed men out by creating worlds exclusively for and by women, in some ways curiously anticipating much of our contemporary Lesbian poetry and novels.

In a certain sense, all of Barney's salon, led by Barney and by the ideas of Vivien (which Barney kept alive after her friend's death in 1909) sought to be disciples of the tenth muse, of the first-known and most respected woman writer, Sappho. In bringing Sappho forward and elevating her to a central position, they were not merely following the lead of their male influences, like Baudelaire and Louÿs, but also giving expression to an intensely felt need to affirm the ancient and inherent power of women to create not just children but an entire world. In recreating the life of Sappho and in reinterpreting her work, they attempted, as did Virginia Woolf in London, "to separate the real Sappho from centuries of scholarly calumny."[2] The declaration of independence from masculine critical standards was a considerable act of daring; perhaps it is demanding too much of Barney, Vivien, or the members of their immediate circle to also ask them to liberate themselves from all previous male influence, to create a wholly new women's literature *ab ovo*.

Yet this is the demand implicit in the criticisms of Vivien which charge her, as Lillian Faderman does,[3] with inauthenticity. The view of Vivien which portrays her as willfully imbibing the poison of Decadent imagery like the eau de cologne which was reputed to have hastened her death misses the point of what she, as well as Natalie Barney, was attempting to do. To Barney and Vivien, the Symbolists were the true modern masters, daring adventurers who had penetrated the areas of the unconscious, of nonreason, of sensibility, where they also felt at home. It was from here, not from previous women writers (except Sappho), that they were convinced that the new sources of women's literature would spring. They did not foresee that, in adapting Symbolist imagery to their own purposes, they would also adopt the attitudes which underlay it, attitudes which were embedded in a male-centered, even misogynist, world-view.

It was their imitation of the male Symbolist writers as well as their French educations which led them to write in French. For Renée Vivien, the choice was simple: From an early age, she had detested her mother tongue, which she associated with her mother and her motherland, England. French was the language of the Symbolists, even though the movement was over by the time she began writing. Furthermore, French was for her, as it was for Barney, a political choice, as it were. French was still the international language of diplomacy, and it allowed them to address the cultured women of the world, in a way that overshadowed the limits of the patriarchal nationalism they so despised.

Barney, though less in thrall to the Symbolists than Vivien, also frequently imitated Baudelaire and Verlaine. She explained, half in jest, in her preface to *Some Portraits and Sonnets of Women* that the French language seemed more poetic than English, in part because English was too familiar to her. She felt she could have no poetic illusions about the words she had used since birth. As a further explanation, she offered the theory that her soul was inhabited by several departed French poets (one can only wonder which ones), and that was the reason her passion for the French language and for France was so strong. She added that neither seemed foreign to her and hoped that some day the compliment would be returned.[4]

Poems, however, were not her forte; her quick, sharp epigrams—her *pensées*—were. The very word *pensées* recalls the names of two French writers, La Bruyère and La Rochefoucauld. Though English writers—Oscar Wilde, for example—used epigrams in their plays, it was the French who truly esteemed a collection of epigrams as a work of art. Yet the decision to write in French was fraught with literary danger which

Barney herself was able to admit.[5] As we have seen, both Barney and Vivien voiced their nontraditional themes in academic formalistic poems and plays in verse. For whatever reason, they did not question the rigid forms as being male or unnecessary; they challenged only the content. As Colette pointed out about Vivien (but it could be said as well of Barney), she was writing in forms that had been fashionable at a much earlier date. Colette correctly attributed this anachronism to their having studied French literature relatively late in life.[6] They found in these French masterpieces a novelty that would be missing for those familiar with the works from early childhood.

In any event, this decision to give up forever not only their native countries but also their native tongue makes Barney and Vivien unique in the canon of women writers. Certainly, other anglophones—Gertrude Stein, for example—stayed abroad through war and peace. But Stein's work is in English, written for other Americans. *The Making of Americans, Three Lives, The Autobiography of Alice B. Toklas, Q.E.D., Fernhurst,* and the libretto for *Four Saints in Three Acts* are all works about Americans. Although Stein borrowed the French Cubist style, she transformed it into an American art form. Her audience, when she found one after all her difficulties obtaining a publisher and recognition, was also American. Barney and Vivien, on the other hand, abandoned patriotism and all the vestiges of their homelands, without seeing perhaps that the French language was not inherently more feminist than their native tongue. And as we have seen, in Barney's case, she embraced Italian Fascism, a patriotism more pernicious than the culture she had abandoned decades earlier.

Barney and Vivien also tried to cast off the restraints of their patriarchal heritage by rejecting the tenets of their Christian heritage. Like their worship of Sappho, the "paganism" they embraced was largely symbolic. It expressed their desire for a liberation from the physical, psychic, and sexual confinements of the post-Victorian world, but it was not a liberation which they were altogether willing to espouse, except symbolically. In company with perhaps the majority of the most radical feminist writers of their day, they were somewhat uncomfortable with the notion of female sensuality. Thus Barney and Vivien were forced to impose a rarefied purity on the Ancient Greeks as well as on the contemporary characters they created. They transformed Aphrodite into a goddess of chastity, and Vivien located Sappho's apotheosis in her ecstatic leap over the cliff. It was the prospect of tremulous, passionate, yet pure sensuousness that attracted Barney and Vivien to the Symbolists and Decadents, and they followed the lead of those pale, glimmering virgins of Baudelaire and Villiers de l'Isle-Adam without recognizing they were on a well-worn path.

Their conviction that men were fully replaceable by women in all areas of human existence was a potentially revolutionary one, but it led them merely to alter the gender of the participants in traditional literary scenarios, without subjecting the resultant relationships to any sort of feminist analysis. From their point of view, the power relationship implicit in the Virgin/page association was perfectly acceptable, as long as women played both parts. If a noble demise qualified the Romantic hero, then female characters had a similar right so to die. A less convention-bound approach might have sought ways in which the female hero could be allowed to live.

Despite all their limitations, it is inaccurate to dismiss Barney and Vivien as "irrelevant"[7] to contemporary feminist writers. Despite their attachment to outmoded literary conventions, despite the failure of their analysis of outworn Romantic associations, they were at base deeply in touch with what might almost be termed a feminist agenda, so uncannily do their preoccupations anticipate those of feminist writers and poets who have come after them but who have not been directly influenced by their work. Except for Vivien's elevation of the primacy of chastity, Barney and Vivien thought the same thoughts, dreamed the same dreams, and undertook the same sort of practical projects that modern feminists have pursued.

Both writers attempted to establish a milieu which would be congenial to themselves and to other women of similar interests. Their literary redemption of Sappho and her circle and their desire to create on the island of Lesbos a Lesbian artists' colony, although poorly conceived and ultimately abortive, sprang from the hope of redeeming what they believed was sacred soil for the creative woman. As such, it was close in spirit to the writings of contemporary Lesbian/feminists. For example, in the 1970s, Jill Johnston suggested the formation of a Lesbian nation,[8] and both she and Monique Wittig, in *Lesbian Body* and *Les Guérillères*, expressed a sense of connection between certain Lesbians that transcends national barriers and geographical separation. As in the stories of Vivien, Wittig creates new and imaginary landscapes for women to inhabit.

In a more immediately practical and effective way, the Academy of Women, established by Barney as an outgrowth of her salon, likewise served to encourage and support women's creativity. In it, women nurtured one another's literary careers by offering constructive criticism of each other's unpublished manuscripts, discussed their mutual difficulties as women writers, and in some cases, were able to offer financial support when necessary. It was also intended as an international forum for French, English, and American women writers. The existence of Barney's Academy may have had a direct influence on the decision of Gloria Orenstein, Erica Duncan, and other women to organize a similar facility in New York City in 1977.

But even more remarkable than Barney's salon and Academy of Women is the degree to which Barney and Vivien both anticipated attitudes toward history, literary themes, and images which also appear throughout contemporary feminist writing. Unlike the majority of their feminist contemporaries, who were concerned with demonstrating their equality with men by minimizing the differences between the sexes, Barney and Vivien were united in recognizing that the separate experience of women profoundly altered their vision of the universe. They would have been in wholehearted agreement with Marguerite Duras, who maintains that in order to create a women's literature it is necessary to "reverse everything. Make women the point of departure in judging, make darkness the point of departure in judging what men call light, make obscurity the point of departure in judging what men call clarity."[9]

This desire to reverse conventional and traditional judgments of significance led Barney and Vivien to search history for examples of female heroes who had been misinterpreted or forgotten by masculinist historians, and to bring them forward once again to serve as models for the present generation. One of the most fruitful areas of contemporary women's studies has been precisely this sort of rediscovery of foremothers, and, indeed, Barney and Vivien themselves are benefiting from the new respectability of feminist studies. But whereas the feminist historian seeks to establish an accurate assessment of her subject, Barney and Vivien were more interested in developing spiritually or poetically viable sources of inspiration. Thus their treatment of Sappho, though from one point of view ahistorical, from another is closely allied to the impulse which led Judy Grahn in *The Highest Apple* to recreate Sappho's life as a woman of greater power and freedom than history would lead us to believe.[10]

The implication is that Sappho may be reinvented in the imagination of the writer and reader. The stance which views all history as ripe for reinterpretation by the poet is ubiquitous in feminist nonfiction, novels, and poetry, when women, such as Andrea Dworkin and Mary Daly, rewrite the history of witches or when novelists, such as Sally Gearhart in *The Wanderground*, make bold acts of identification with them. Others—for instance, Suzy McKee Charnas in *Motherlines*—have created futuristic tales of Amazons. Single women, often denigrated in masculinist literature, have found their place in contemporary feminist fiction. In May Sarton's *The Small Room*, "Rachel Vinrace and Mary Datchet choose death and a celibate singlehood over the alternative of marriage,"[11] in a way that Vivien would have found most congenial.

Barney and Vivien's attempt to deliver a religion which would at once serve the needs of a woman's imagination and avoid the generally anti-woman strictures of patriarchal religion also strikes a consonant chord with contemporary feminists (for example, Z. Budapest and Merlin Stone). Although large numbers of women attempt to reanimate a version of the religion of the Great Mother of the pre-Classical era, or a feminist version of medieval witchcraft called Wicca, still others are, like Barney and Vivien, concerned with revitalizing the Classical goddesses, at least as sources of poetic imagery. In their entry on "Diana," Wittig and Zeig label her ". . . the only known amazon goddess to whom all the lesbian peoples remained attached after the time of the amazons, writing poems and celebrations in her name. . . . Each of those eager to rejoin the dispersed amazons consecrated her daughter to Diana."[12] However, no one appears to have followed Vivien in her attempt to convert Aphrodite into a goddess of chastity.

The gynandrous future envisioned by Barney and Vivien is also widely encountered in feminist writing, though it is perhaps less commonly embraced than is the revisionist attitude toward history and myth. The notion most frequently surfaces in speculative and visionary fiction, like Joanna Russ's *The Female Man*, Ursula Le Guin's *The Dispossessed*, or Sally Gearhart's *The Wanderground*. The concept of the end result of an evolutionary process which would render gender irrelevant takes the form most frequently of the invention of a new gynandrous being who, like those imagined by both Barney and Vivien, is more female than male in essence. Thus, two women mate in Joanna Russ's *The Female Man*, while the neuter pronoun invented to mask the genders of the characters in June Arnold's *The Cook and the Carpenter*, when finally dropped, reveals them to have been women all along. The evolution of the gynandromorph appears to these writers, as it did to Barney and Vivien, as a way of overcoming the persistence of stereotypical gender descriptions and the resultant inequalities which arise from them. As Andrea Dworkin observes in *Woman Hating:*

> The discovery is, of course, that "man" and "woman" are fictions, caricatures, cultural constructs. As models, they are reductive, totalitarian, inappropriate to human becoming. As roles they are static, demeaning to the female, dead-ended for male and female both. . . . [The] mythological image [of the androgyne] is a paradigm for a wholeness, a harmony, and a freedom which is virtually unimaginable, the antithesis of every assumption we hold about the nature of identity in general and sex in particular.[13]

Much of the working out of Barney's forthright and unapologetic defense of Lesbianism has occurred in the area of political theory, but it has only been roughly from 1970 that both poets and novelists have felt comfortable with expressing attitudes that Barney adopted fifty years ago and more. In the mid-seventies, Monique Wittig and Adrienne Rich wrote unequivocal Lesbian love poetry in *Lesbian Body* and *Twenty-One Love Poems,* respectively. Even more to the point, Rich objected when told by heterosexual friends, who presumably intended a compliment, that her poetry was "universal."[14] But Rich is perhaps the first poet since Natalie Barney to have done so and retained a large audience and mainstream publication. Amy Lowell and Hilda Doolittle had found it expedient to alter pronouns and strive for the universality which Adrienne Rich and, before her, Natalie Barney and Renée Vivien had forsworn.

Approximately eighty years after the fruitful association between Natalie Barney and Renée Vivien, it has become possible to judge the nature and the importance of what they were attempting to do. For decades both had been the object of trivialization which had the effect, whether intentional or not, of reducing them to a literary sideshow, in which context the radical element in their work could be viewed as an expression of their fundamental extremism, and thus not worthy of serious consideration. Unquestionably, both were seriously flawed. The very privilege which made their lives possible was also a shield, especially in the case of Barney, against the necessity to take herself as seriously as she ought and as her work required. Their indebtedness to the Symbolists and Decadents was the expression of their conviction that they were fully able to compete with those whom they believed to be the masters of modern French poetry; however, that adherence doomed them to stylistic imitation from which Vivien, in particular, never succeeded in freeing herself, perhaps because she died so young.

Nevertheless, beneath the slightly tattered flutterings of Vivien's and Barney's post-Romantic and Symbolist imagery and beyond the stylized, theatrical posturing of the Virgin and the page, we find two poets consumed with the vision of the prospect of a new, free woman, who would act and live boldly and independently of men. The new woman they created could look back to Lilith and Vashti for historical precedents of defiant behavior and to the reconstructed Sappho for intellectual independence. The female hero roamed in a fictional wilderness, where man dared to follow her only at his own risk. She was capable of rising to a gynandrous completeness that offered her freedom from the routine expectations imposed upon the woman of the early twentieth century, such as marriage and childbearing. Because of their unapologetic visions of what women were and what women could be, they made it more possible for other contemporary writers to expand the potentials of female characters. By creating bold dreams of female autonomy and by occasionally attempting to reify them in their lives, Barney and Vivien have created for themselves a permanent place as genuine foremothers of modern feminist literature.

NOTES

Introduction

1. Natalie Clifford Barney, *Aventures de l'esprit* (Paris, 1929; New York: Arno, 1975), pp. 253–54. All translations from the French are by Karla Jay, unless an English edition is noted. The translations of the poetry are meant to be literal rather than lyrical.

2. Natalie Clifford Barney, *Souvenirs indiscrets* (Paris: Flammarion, 1960), p. 25.

3. François Chapon et al. *Autour de Natalie Clifford Barney* (Paris: Universités de Paris, 1976), p. 10.

4. This information was related to me by Jean Chalon in Paris in July 1978.

I. The Amazon and the Page

1. Various figures are given for the amount of Barney's inheritance. George Wickes estimates it at two and a half million dollars, but Shari Benstock notes that another million and a half was given to each daughter by Alice Pike Barney before she remarried. See George Wickes, *The Amazon of Letters: The Life and Loves of Natalie Barney* (New York: Putnam's, 1976), p. 20, and Shari Benstock, *Women of the Left Bank, Paris, 1900–1940* (Austin: University of Texas Press, 1986), p. 269.

2. Natalie Clifford Barney, "Nos secrètes amours," MS, fols. 84–85. All manuscripts by Natalie Barney and letters to and from her are from the Bibliothèque Doucet, Paris.

3. Natalie Clifford Barney, *Souvenirs indiscrets* (Paris: Flammarion, 1960), p. 29.

4. Barney, "Secrètes," fol. 58.

5. Olivia [Dorothy Strachey], *Olivia* (New York: Sloane, 1949).

6. Barney, "Secrètes," fol. 30.

7. Barney, "Secrètes," fol. 233.

8. Barney, *Souvenirs*, p. 43.

9. Lord Alfred Douglas's notoriety followed him long after the death of his lover, Oscar Wilde.

10. Benstock, p. 271.

11. Wickes, pp. 46–47.

12. Benstock, p. 273.

13. Alice Pike Barney, letter to Natalie Clifford Barney, 25 January 1901, fol. 1.

14. Barney frequently used these words to refer to herself in unpublished letters and plays.

15. Natalie Clifford Barney, letters to Alice Pike Barney, 1901–1919.

16. Renée O'Brien, letter to Karla Jay, 23 April 1986.

17. O'Brien, letter.

18. O'Brien, letter.

19. Renée Vivien, letter to Amédée Moullé, 21 May 1894, fol. 117. Letters to Amédée Moullé 1894–1895, Bibliothèque Nationale, Paris. Most of the following

account is based on Vivien's own recollections of her childhood as told in letters to Moullé.

20. Vivien, Moullé, 8 August 1894, fol. 173.

21. Vivien, Moullé, 22 May 1894, fol. 123.

22. Personal interview with Renée O'Brien, 6 January 1986. Moullé was married, but that did not deter him from pursuing an heiress.

23. Renée Vivien, Moullé, n.d., fol. 191. This letter probably dates from late autumn 1894.

24. Jean-Paul Goujon, *Tes blessures sont plus douces que leurs caresses* (Paris: Desforges, 1986), p. 34.

25. Gertrude Stein, *Paris France* (New York: Liveright, 1970), pp. 119–20.

26. Natalie Clifford Barney, *Souvenirs indiscrets* (Paris: Flammarion, 1960), p. 21.

27. Although Renée Vivien and perhaps some of the other female expatriates at that time were not actively Lesbians, they most likely felt a sense of being "different."

28. Natalie Clifford Barney, *Poems & poèmes: autres alliances* (Paris: Emile-Paul; New York: Doran, 1920), p. 18. This work is half in English, half in French. The title is the word for "poem" in each language.

29. Karla Jay, "Male Homosexuality and Lesbianism in the Works of Proust and Gide," in *The Gay Academic*, ed. Louie Crew (Palm Springs, Cal.: Etc., 1978), pp. 216–43.

30. Renée Vivien, *Une Femme m'apparut* . . . (1904; rpt. Paris: Desforges, 1977), p. 29.

31. Radclyffe Hall, *The Well of Loneliness* (New York: Pocket,1974), p. 246.

32. Barney, *Souvenirs*, pp. 43–44. The same description may be found in "Secrètes," fols. 249–50.

33. Colette, *The Pure and the Impure* (New York: Farrar Straus, 1967), p. 80.

34. Vivien, *Femme*, passim. Details were extrapolated from the novel.

35. Gayle Rubin, Introd., *A Woman Appeared to Me* by Renée Vivien (Reno, Nev.: Naiad, 1976), p. xx.

36. Renée Vivien, "Mensonge du soir," *A l'heure des mains jointes* (1906) in *Poèmes de Renée Vivien*, Vol II (Paris, 1923; rpt. New York: Arno, 1975), p. 103; hereinafter referred to as *PRV* I or II.

37. Tryphé [Natalie Clifford Barney], *Cinq petits dialogues grecs (antithèses et parallèles)* (Paris: Plume, 1902), pp. 11–44.

38. Tryphé, p. 33.

39. Barney, "Secrètes," fol. 260.

40. Vivien, *Femme*, p. 108. Italics in original.

41. Vivien, *Femme*, p. 109.

42. Vivien, *Femme*, p. 29.

43. Barney, *Souvenirs*, p. 64.

44. Barney, *Souvenirs*, pp. 64–67. Once, for example, Vivien refused to dine with the poet Olive Custance because she was English.

45. Barney, *Souvenirs*, p. 72.

46. Barney, *Souvenirs*, p. 73.

47. Barney, *Souvenirs*, p. 76.

48. Barney, *Souvenirs*, p. 76.

49. Barney, *Souvenirs*, p. 77.

50. In a poem written around 1904, Vivien refers to Lesbos as an escape from persecution as well as a positive destination for Lesbians.

51. Renée Vivien, "Atthis," *Evocations* (1903) in *PRV* I, p. 79.

52. Renée Vivien, "Les Vents," *Brumes de fjords* (Paris: Lemerre, 1902), pp. 7–12.

53. Renée Vivien, "Les Deux Amours," *Brumes*, p. 49.

54. Paul Lorenz, *Sapho 1900, Renée Vivien* (Paris: Julliard, 1977), p. 91.

55. Quoted by Simone Burgues in letter to Karla Jay, 24 August 1985, fol. 2.

56. Burgues, fol. 2.

57. Burgues, fol. 2.

58. Colette, pp. 81–82.

59. Colette, p. 95. Italics in original.

60. Colette, p. 95.

61. Colette, pp. 88–89.

62. Sandra M. Gilbert and Susan Gubar, *The Madwoman in the Attic: The Woman Writer and the Nineteenth Century Literary Imagination* (New Haven: Yale University Press, 1979), pp. 286 & 297.

63. Gilbert and Gubar, p. 391.

64. Barney, "Secrètes," fol. 337.

65. André Germain, *Renée Vivien* (Paris: Crès, 1917).

66. Renée Vivien, "Ainsi je parlerai . . ." *Heure* in *PRV* II, p. 52.

67. Natalie Clifford Barney, "La Mort du poète," in *Actes et entr'actes* (Paris: Sansot, 1910), p. 235.

68. Natalie Clifford Barney, *Aventures de l'esprit* (Paris, 1929; rpt. New York: Arno, 1975), p. 257.

69. Barney, "La Chambre vide," in *Actes*, p. 99.

70. Barney, "Nous irons vers les poètes," in *Actes*, p. 238.

71. Personal interview with Berthe Cleyrergue, 20 July 1978.

72. Barney, "Nous irons," p. 238.

73. Barney, "La Double mort," *Actes*, pp. 20–43.

II. Staying On, but Never Alone

1. George Wickes, *The Amazon of Letters: The Life and Loves of Natalie Barney* (New York: Putnam's, 1976), p. 104.

2. Quoted in Wickes, p. 9.

3. Natalie Clifford Barney, *Nouvelles pensées de l'amazone* (Paris: Mercure de France, 1939), p. 49.

4. Gayle Rubin, Slide show and talk on Natalie Barney and Renée Vivien, Oscar Wilde '84 Conference, Toronto, Ont., 1–5 July 1984.

5. Natalie Clifford Barney, *Aventures de l'esprit* (Paris: 1929; rpt. New York; Arno, 1975), p. 274.

6. André Rouveyre, *Souvenirs de mon commerce* (Paris: Crès, 1921), pp. 66–67.

7. Rouveyre, p. 42.

8. Rouveyre, p. 72.

9. Remy de Gourmont, *Lettres intimes à l'amazone*. 4th ed. (Paris: La Centaine, 1927), p. 151.

10. Remy de Gourmont, *Lettres à l'amazone*. 18th ed. (Paris: Crès, 1922), p. 186.

11. The relationship also brings to mind the distant, icy woman of Mallarmé's *Hérodiade*.

12. Rouveyre, p. 85.

13. William Carlos Williams, *The Autobiography of William Carlos Williams* (New York: Random, 1951), p. 229.

14. Gourmont, *Lettres intimes*, p. 258.

15. Gourmont, *Lettres intimes*, p. 253.

16. Alice Pike Barney, letter to Natalie Clifford Barney, 14 July 1924, fol. 1. All manuscripts by and letters to Natalie Barney are from the Bibliothèque Doucet, Paris.

17. Quoted in *The Los Angeles Record*, 13 April 1925, p. 2.

18. Natalie Clifford Barney, *Pensées d'une amazone* (Paris: Emile-Paul, 1920), p. 6.

19. Shari Benstock, *Women of the Left Bank, Paris, 1900–1940* (Austin: University of Texas Press, 1986), p. 296.

20. Barney, *Pensées*, p. 31.

21. Barney, *Pensées*, p. 21.

22. Barney, *Pensées*, p. 22.

23. Meryle Secrest, *Between Me and Life: A Biography of Romaine Brooks* (Garden City, N.Y.: Doubleday, 1974), pp. 135–36.

24. Romaine Brooks, *Thief of Souls* (Washington, D.C.: National Collection of Fine Arts, 1971).

25. Barney, *Aventures*, p. 247.

26. Barney, *Aventures*, pp. 245–46.

27. Benstock, p. 304.

28. Romaine Brooks, *Self-Portrait*, National Collection of Fine Arts, Washington, D.C.

29. Secrest, passim.

30. Adelyn D. Breeskin, ed. *Romaine Brooks* (Washington, D.C.: Smithsonian, 1986), p. 105.

31. Quoted in Wickes, p. 183.

32. Wickes, pp. 166–67.

33. Wickes, p. 167.

34. Karla Jay, "Decoding the *Ladies Almanack*," paper for a special session on "Djuna Barnes: A Renaissance," Modern Language Association, 29 December 1982, Los Angeles, Cal.

35. Personal interview with Ned Rorem, 29 October 1983.

36. Karla Jay, "The Amazon Was a Pacifist," in *Reweaving the Web of Life: Feminism and Nonviolence*, ed. Pam McAllister (Philadelphia: New Society, 1982), pp. 101–105.

37. Natalie Clifford Barney, "Amazon's Note-Book," MS, fol. 60. The date of this notebook is approximately 1940.

III. Gynocentricity

1. Gertrude Stein, *Fernhurst* in *Fernhurst, Q.E.D. and Other Early Writings* (New York: Liveright, 1971), pp. 4–5.

2. Quoted in Lillian Faderman, *Surpassing the Love of Men* (New York: Morrow, 1981), p. 371.

3. Mary Barnard, *Sappho: A New Translation* (Berkeley: University of California Press, 1958), frag. 60.

4. Renée Vivien, "Vous pour qui j'écrivis," *A l'heure des mains jointes* (1906) in *Poèmes de Renée Vivien*, 2 vols. (Paris, 1923; rpt. New York: Arno, 1975), pp. 110–11; hereinafter cited as *PRV* I or *PRV* II. Another version, for example, appears in *Sapho* (1903), p. 149.

5. Renée Vivien, "Voici ce que je chanterai," *Flambeaux éteints* (1908), in *PRV* II, p. 187.

6. This shift to an imagined female audience is noticeable in the later work of

Adrienne Rich, for example, as well as made overt by the inscription "For women only" which appears on the covers of some Lesbian/feminist collections of poetry.

7. Natalie Clifford Barney, *Pensées d'une amazone* (Paris: Emile-Paul, 1920), p. 151.

8. Renée Vivien, "Les Succubes disent . . ." *La Vénus des aveugles* (1903), in *PRV* I, p. 196.

9. Vivien, "Succubes," p. 197.

10. Renée Vivien, "Union," *Sillages* (1908), in *PRV* II, p. 162. Ellipsis in original.

11. Renée Vivien, "Litanie de la haine," *Vénus* (1906), in *PRV* I, p. 217.

12. Renée Vivien, "Souveraines," *Evocations* (1903), in *PRV* I, pp. 100–104.

13. Natalie Clifford Barney, "Nos secrètes amours," MS, fol. 52. All manuscripts are undated and are from the Bibliothèque Doucet, Paris.

14. Renée Vivien, *Une Femme m'apparut. . .* (1904; rpt. Paris: Desforges, 1977), p. 58. During this conversation between San Giovanni and the narrator, the former claims to have rewritten the story of Vashti found in *The Woman of the Wolf*, demonstrating how closely Vivien identified with some of her characters and what little distinction she seemed to draw between life and fiction.

15. Renée Vivien, "The Veil of Vashti," *The Woman of the Wolf* (1904; rpt. New York: Gay Presses of New York, 1983), p. 76. Ellipsis in original.

16. The characterization of the slave woman as fearful and abject has unfortunate anti-Semitic overtones, especially in post-Dreyfus Paris, though elsewhere, Vivien expressed a high regard for the Jewish people.

17. Vivien, "The Veil," p. 73.

18. Vivien, "The Veil," p. 79.

19. Sandra M. Gilbert and Susan Gubar, *The Madwoman in the Attic: The Woman Writer and the Nineteenth Century Literary Imagination* (New Haven: Yale University Press, 1979), p. 35.

20. Vivien, "The Veil," p. 73.

21. As we shall see in Chapter 5, many of these same traits are attributed to the figure of the decadent Virgin.

22. Vivien, "Souveraines," pp. 100–101.

23. Renée Vivien, "The Woman of the Wolf," *Woman*, p. 8.

24. Vivien, "Woman," p. 9. Ellipsis in original.

25. Renée Vivien, "The Nut-Brown Maid," *Woman*, p. 86.

26. Vivien, "Maid," p. 83.

27. Vivien, "Maid," p. 89. Ellipses in original.

28. Vivien, "Maid," p. 89.

29. Annis Pratt, *Archetypal Patterns in Women's Fiction* (Bloomington: Indiana University Press, 1981), p. 17.

30. Karla Jay, Introd., *Woman*, p. vi.

31. Renée Vivien, "Snickering Thirst," *Woman*, p. 17.

32. Vivien, "Thirst," p. 17.

33. Pratt, p. 19.

34. Pratt, p. 126.

35. Renée Vivien, "The Crocodile Lady," *Woman*, p. 68.

36. Vivien, "Crocodile," p. 71. Ellipsis in original.

37. Pratt, p. 119.

38. Jean-Paul Goujon, "Un Livre inédit de Renée Vivien: *Anne Boleyn,*" *Bulletin du Bibliophile* II (1977), 144.

39. Renée Vivien, *Anne Boleyn: Reproduction en fac-similé des épreuves uniques de l'édition jamais tirée de Lemerre (1909)* (Muizon: L'Ecart, 1982), p. 71.

40. Vivien, *Boleyn*, p. 47.

41. Vivien, *Boleyn*, p. 50. Italics and English in original.

42. Vivien, *Boleyn*, p. 21.

43. Vivien, *Boleyn*, p. 22.

44. Renée Vivien, "White as Foam," *Woman*, p. 114.

45. Vivien, "Foam," p. 115.

46. Vivien, "Foam," p. 114.

47. Vivien, *Femme*, p. 141. Ellipses in original.

48. Vivien, *Femme*, p. 26. Italics in original.

49. Vivien, *Femme*, p. 103.

50. Pratt, p. 25.

51. Renée Vivien, "Nous irons vers les poètes," *Heures*, in *PRV* II, p. 57. Ellipses in original.

52. Barney, *Pensées*, pp. 1–52.

53. Since Barney's plays are undated, it is difficult to ascertain whether the epigrams first appeared in the plays or in her three volumes of *pensées*. Also, since most of her plays are in English, and all her *pensées* are in French, there are sometimes slight differences in lines, due to translation.

54. Natalie Clifford Barney, "Autour d'une victoire," *Actes et entr'actes* (Paris: Sansot, 1910), p. 221. This play should not be confused with an unpublished play, bearing the same title, in the Bibliothèque Doucet.

55. Barney, *Pensées*, p. 18. Ellipsis in original.

56. Barney, *Pensées*, p. 139.

57. Natalie Clifford Barney, "Le Mystère de Psyché," MS, fol. 20.

58. Barney, *Pensées*, p. 17.

59. Barney, *Pensées*, p. 9.

60. Barney, *Pensées*, p. 97.

61. Liane de Pougy, *Mes cahiers bleus* (Paris: Plon, 1977), p. 281. The journal entry dates from 1933. De Pougy, in her life and in *Idylle saphique*, called Barney "Flossie."

62. Renée Vivien, "Je t'aime d'être faible . . ." (1906), *Heure*, in *PRV* II, p. 66.

63. Renée Vivien, "Mains sur un front de malade," *Dans un coin de violettes* (1910), in *PRV* II, p. 217. Ellipses in original.

64. Jean Venettis, "Renée Vivien et l'idéal païen (I)," *Revue palladienne* No. 2 (1948), p. 48.

65. Irving Brown, *Leconte de Lisle: A Study of the Man and His Poetry* (New York: AMS Press, 1966), p. 171.

66. Brown, pp. 171–72.

67. Quoted in Brown, p. 174.

68. Natalie Clifford Barney, "Seins," *Traits et portraits* (1963; rpt. New York: Arno, 1975), p. 184.

69. Natalie Clifford Barney, "La Belle aux désirs dormants," *Quelques portraits-sonnets de femmes* (Paris: Société d'Editions littéraires, 1900), p. 5.

70. Quoted in George Wickes, *The Amazon of Letters: The Life and Loves of Natalie Barney* (New York: Putnam's, 1976), p. 15.

71. Joanna Russ, "What Can a Heroine Do? Or Why Women Can't Write," in *Images of Women in Fiction: Feminist Perspectives*, ed. Susan Koppelman Cornillon (Bowling Green: Bowling Green University Popular Press, 1972), pp. 4–5.

72. Russ, p. 7.

73. Russ, p. 9.

74. Russ, p. 11.

75. Russ, pp. 10–11.
76. Jay, p. ii.
77. Jay, p. iii.

IV. Sappho and Other Goddesses

1. David M. Robinson, *Sappho and Her Influence* (New York: Cooper Square, 1963), p. 134.
2. Susan Gubar, "Sapphistries," *Signs,* 10 (1984), 46–47.
3. Robinson, pp. 35–41.
4. Natalie Clifford Barney, *Aventures de l'esprit* (Paris, 1929; rpt. New York: Arno, 1975), p. 21.
5. Pierre Louÿs, *Les Chansons de Bilitis,* in *Oeuvres complètes,* III (Geneva: Slatkine, 1973), pp. 63–111.
6. Natalie Clifford Barney, "Nos secrètes amours," MS, fol. 102. All manuscripts and letters are from the Bibliothèque Doucet, Paris. All manuscripts are undated.
7. Yves-Gérard Le Dantec, *Renée Vivien: femme damnée, femme sauvée* (Aix-en-Provence: Editions du Feu, 1930), pp. 155–56.
8. Alex Preminger, ed. *Princeton Encyclopedia of Poetry and Poetics,* Enlarged ed. (Princeton: Princeton University Press, 1974), p. 737.
9. Algernon Charles Swinburne, "Sapphics," *Poems and Ballads* (First Series), in *The Works of Algernon Charles Swinburne: Poems* (Philadelphia: McKay, n.d.), p. 82.
10. Henri Monier, *Dictionnaire de poétique et de rhétorique* (Paris: Presses universitaires de France, 1961), c.v.
11. Le Dantec, pp. 156–57.
12. Gubar, p. 46.
13. George Wickes, *The Amazon of Letters: The Life and Loves of Natalie Barney* (New York: Putnam's, 1976), p. 59.
14. Barney, "Secrètes," fols. 252–53.
15. Renée Vivien, *Une Femme m'apparut . . .* (1904; rpt. Paris: Desforges, 1977), p. 40.
16. Gubar, p. 47.
17. Renée Vivien, "Sonnet," *Etudes et préludes* (1901) in *Poèmes de Renée Vivien.* 2 vols. (Paris, 1923; rpt. New York: Arno, 1975), p. 33; hereafter cited as *PRV* I or *PRV* II.
18. Renée Vivien, "Psappha revit," *A l'Heure des mains jointes* (1906), in *PRV* II, pp. 50–51.
19. Jean Venettis, "Renée Vivien et l'idéal païen (I)," *Revue palladienne,* No. 2 (May–June 1948), p. 49.
20. Ovid, "The Heroides XV," *Heroides and Amores,* 2nd ed., I (Cambridge: Harvard University Press, 1977), pp. 180–97.
21. Richard F. Burton, "Terminal Essay," *A Plain and Literal Translation of the Arabian Nights Entertainments* (Benares, India: Kamahastra Society, 1885), p. x.
22. Barney, "Secrètes," fol. 42.
23. Natalie Clifford Barney, "Equivoque," *Actes et entr'actes* (Paris: Sansot, 1910), p. 81.
24. Natalie Clifford Barney, "Le Mystère de Psyché," MS, fol. 29.
25. Vivien, *Femme,* p. 38.
26. Vivien, *Femme,* p. 38.

27. Renée Vivien, "La Sirène muette," *Brumes de fjords* (Paris: Lemerre, 1902), p. 86.

28. Edith Mora, *Sappho: histoire d'un poète et traduction intégrale de l'oeuvre* (Paris: Flammarion, 1966), pp. 199–200. Lucie Delarue-Mardrus wrote *Sapho désespérée* (1905), which performed at the Théâtre Antique d'Orange but which was never published. Natalie Barney provided the costumes. Mora, p. 198.

29. Monique Wittig and Sande Zeig. *Lesbian Peoples: Material for a Dictionary* (New York: Avon, 1979), p. 136.

30. Renée Vivien, "La Mort de Psappha," *Evocations*, in *PRV* I, p. 89. In "Atthis délaissée," p. 121, Vivien identifies with Atthis, who says, *"Je t'aimais au long des lointaines années . . ."* and who is dying of unrequited love for Sappho. In general, however, Vivien's identification is with Sappho.

31. Vivien, "La Mort," p. 91. Italics in original.

32. Vivien, "La Mort," p. 92.

33. Vivien, "La Mort," p. 93.

34. Vivien, "La Mort," p. 93.

35. Vivien, *Femme*, p. 38.

36. Mary Daly, *Beyond God the Father: Toward a Philosophy of Women's Liberation* (Boston: Beacon, 1973), p. 8.

37. Tryphé [Natalie Clifford Barney], *Cinq petits dialogues grecs (antithèses et parallèles)* (Paris: Plume, 1902), pp. 17–21.

38. Barney, "Equivoque," p. 60.

39. Le Dantec, pp. 184–85.

40. Gubar, p. 49

41. Renée Vivien, "Dans un verger," *Sillages* (1908), in *PRV* II, pp. 142–43.

42. Renée Vivien, "Invocation," *Cendres et poussières* (1902), in *PRV* I, p. 44.

43. Renée Vivien, *Les Kitharèdes* (1904), in *PRV* II, p. 31.

44. Renée Vivien, "Les Oliviers," *La Vénus des aveugles* (1903), in *PRV* I, p. 207.

45. Renée Vivien, "Bona Dea," *The Woman of the Wolf* (1904; rpt. New York: Gay Presses of New York, 1983), p. 118.

46. Vivien, *Kitharèdes*, p. 32.

47. Wickes, p. 59.

48. Barney, "Secrètes," fols. 184–85.

49. Natalie Clifford Barney, letter to Alice Pike Barney, n.d. This letter probably dates from Lesbos, 1904.

50. Monique Wittig, *The Lesbian Body* (New York: Morrow, 1975), p. 26. That Wittig is thinking less of the actual islands of Lesbos and Cythera than of their historical and mythic reverberations is suggested by the fact that she pluralizes both place names in the original French—that is "les Lesbos."

51. Erich Neumann, *The Great Mother: An Analysis of the Archetype* (Princeton: Princeton University Press, 1974), passim.

52. Vivien. *Femme*, p. 56.

53. H. J. Rose, *A Handbook of Greek Mythology Including Its Extension to Rome* (New York: Dutton, 1959), p. 326.

54. Colette, *La Vagabonde* in *Œuvres complètes de Colette*, III (Paris: Flammarion, 1973), pp. 382–83.

55. Mary Barnard, *Sappho: A New Translation* (Berkeley: University of California Press, 1958), frag. 38.

56. Barney, *Dialogues grecs*, p. 10.

57. J. E. Cirlot, *A Dictionary of Symbols*, 2nd ed. (New York: Philosophical Library, 1978), pp. 364–65.

58. Dianne F. Sadoff, "Mythopoeia, the Moon and Contemporary Women's Poetry," in *Feminist Criticism: Essays on Theory, Poetry and Prose,* ed. Cheryl L. Brown and Karen Olson (Metuchen, N.J.: Scarecrow, 1978), p. 157.

59. Renée Vivien, "La Nuit est à nous . . ." (1903), *Evocations,* in *PRV* I, p. 104.

60. Vivien, *Femme,* pp. 40–41.

61. Renée Vivien, "Enseignement" (1908), *Sillages,* in *PRV* II, p. 159. Ellipsis in original.

62. Vivien, "Enseignement," p. 159.

63. Barney, *Dialogues grecs,* p. 26.

64. Renée Vivien, "Les Fleurs de Séléné" (1902), *Cendres,* in *PRV* I, p. 56.

65. Renée Vivien, "Incipit Liber Veneris Caecorum" (1903), *Vénus,* in *PRV* I, p. 183.

66. Renée Vivien, "Velléda" (1903), *Evocations,* in *PRV* I, p. 111.

67. Barney, *Dialogues grecs,* p. 26.

68. Renée Vivien, "La Mort de Psappha," *Evocations,* p. 91.

69. Vivien, "Enseignement", p. 159. Vivien uses the same expression, "âme solitaire," in "Fleurs de Séléné" (1902).

70. Renée Vivien, "J'enseignai les chants à la vierge aux pieds d'or," (1903), *Sapho,* in *PRV* I, p. 174.

71. Renée Vivien, "La Sirène muette" *Brumes,* p. 87.

72. Barney, "Mystère," MS, fol. 3.

73. Barney, "Mystère," fol. 3.

74. Barney, "Mystère," fol. 3.

75. Renée Vivien, "The Woman of the Wolf," *Woman,* p. 9.

76. Renée Vivien, "Erôs, de tes mains prodigues de douleurs" (1903), *Sapho,* p. 178.

77. Renée Vivien, "Verger," pp. 104–12.

78. Natalie Clifford Barney, "Autour d'une victoire," in *Actes,* p. 190.

79. Natalie Clifford Barney, *Eparpillements* (Paris: Sansot, 1910), p. 61.

V. The Religion of Love

1. Marina Warner, *Alone of All Her Sex: The Myth and the Cult of the Virgin Mary* (London: Quartet, 1978), p. 282.

2. Edwin Oliver James, *The Cult of the Mother Goddess: An Archaeological and Documentary Study* (New York: Praeger, 1959), passim.

3. Robert Graves, *The Greek Myths* I (Baltimore: Penguin, 1955), p. 50.

4. An interesting recent novelistic treatment of this conflict may be found in Marian Zimmer Bradley, *The Mists of Avalon* (New York: Knopf, 1983).

5. Renée Vivien, *Une Femme m'apparut . . .* (1904; rpt. Paris: Desforges, 1977), p. 114.

6. Renée Vivien, "Notre-Dame des Fièvres" (1904), Intro. to *Poèmes de Renée Vivien* II (Paris, 1923; rpt. New York: Arno, 1975), p. 1. Ellipsis in original. The poems are hereafter cited as *PRV* I or *PRV* II. A parenthetical cross-reference at the bottom of the poem refers the reader to *A Woman Appeared to Me,* where the poem is attributed to San Giovanni (p. 114). That Vivien interchanges herself without explanation with San Giovanni underscores her identification with the character.

7. Natalie Clifford Barney, *Nouvelles pensées de l'amazone* (Paris: Mercure de France, 1939), p. 56. Although published as late as 1939, Barney collected her *éparpillements* ("scatterings") over many years, starting in 1900. A sample of her *pensées* was first published in 1920 as *Pensées d'une amazone.*

8. Bertha Harris, "The More Profound Nationality of Their Lesbianism: Lesbian Society in Paris in the 1920's," in *Amazon Expedition: A Lesbianfeminist Anthology,* ed. Phyllis Birkby et al. (New York: Times Change Press, 1973), pp. 86–87.

9. Natalie Clifford Barney, "Salle des pas perdus," MS, fol. 20. All manuscripts and letters are from the Bibliothèque Doucet, Paris. None of her manuscripts is dated.

10. Natalie Clifford Barney, "Nos secrètes amours," MS, fol. 293.

11. Renée Vivien, "Sans fleurs à votre front. . . ." *A l'heure des mains jointes* (1906), in *PRV* II, p. 79.

12. Renée Vivien, "Le Pilori," *Heure,* p. 112. These two poems, dating from 1906, again contradict the commonly held misconception that Vivien concerned herself with Christian imagery only during the last year of her life (1909).

13. Vivien, "Pilori," p. 112.

14. See, for example, Rosemary Curb and Nancy Manahan, eds., *Lesbian Nuns: Breaking Silence* (Tallahassee, Fl.: Naiad, 1985).

15. Vivien, *Femme,* p. 117. Italics in the original.

16. Vivien, *Femme,* p. 117. Italics in the original.

17. Susan Gubar, "Sapphistries," *Signs,* 10 (1984), 49.

18. Renée Vivien, "Amazone," *Etudes et préludes* (1901), in *PRV* I, p. 38. Although Barney was called "L'Amazone," this poem does not seem to refer to her.

19. Renée Vivien, "Let the Dead bury their Dead," *Cendres et poussières* (1902), in *PRV* I, p. 44.

20. Renée Vivien, "Regard en arrière," *Sillages* (1908), in *PRV* II, p. 147.

21. Renée Vivien, "La Légende de Saule," in *Brumes de fjords* (Paris: Lemerre, 1902), p. 103. Ellipsis in original. This is basically a prose poem.

22. Renée Vivien, "Devant le couchant" (1908), *Sillages,* p. 163.

23. Renée Vivien, "Appel," *Haillons* (1910), in *PRV* II, p. 253. Ellipses in original.

24. Renée Vivien, "Dans les lendemains . . ." *Sapho* (1903), in *PRV* I, p. 167. Vivien used this line, with minor variations, in a number of places, including "Pour une," *La Vénus des aveugles* (1903), in *PRV* I, p. 219.

25. Renée Vivien, "Mes victoires" (1906), *Heure,* p. 74.

26. Natalie Clifford Barney, "Sonnet XIII," *Quelques portraits-sonnets de femmes* (Paris: Société d'Editions littéraires, 1900), p. 19.

27. Quoted in Gayle Rubin, Introd. *A Woman Appeared to Me* by Renée Vivien (Reno, Nev.: Naiad, 1976), p. xxi.

28. Natalie Clifford Barney, "Sonnet," *Actes et entr'actes* (Paris: Sansot, 1910), p. 237.

29. C. S. Lewis, *The Allegory of Love: A Study in Medieval Tradition* (London: Oxford University Press, 1938), p. 25.

30. Natalie Clifford Barney, "Le Mystère de Psyché," MS, fol. 6.

31. Remy de Gourmont, *Lettres à l'amazone.* 18th ed. (Paris: Crès, 1922), p. 54.

32. Vivien, *Femme,* p. 104.

33. Barney, *Nouvelles pensées,* p. 108.

34. Renée Vivien, "A la femme aimée," *Etudes,* p. 5. Italics in original.

35. Warner, p. 136.

36. Vivien, *Femme,* p. 30.

37. Vivien, *Femme,* p. 72.

38. Liane de Pougy, *Idylle saphique* (Paris: Plume, 1901), p. 23. Ellipses in original. Though signed by de Pougy, this work was the product of a collaboration between Barney and de Pougy.

39. Renée Vivien, "La Maison du passé" (1908), *Sillages,* p. 169.

40. Vivien, *Femme*, p. 152.

41. Renée Vivien, "Pour le lys," *Dans un coin de violettes* (1910), in *PRV* II, p. 218.

42. Barney, "Secrètes," fol. 182.

43. Jane Marcus, "The Niece of a Nun: Virginia Woolf, Caroline Stephen, and the Cloistered Imagination," in *Virginia Woolf: A Feminist Slant*, ed. Jane Marcus (Lincoln: University of Nebraska Press, 1984), p. 7.

44. Lewis, p. 2.

45. Warner, p. 138.

46. Barney, *Nouvelles pensées*, p. 189.

47. Vivien, *Femme*, p. 131.

48. Renée Vivien, "La Douve," *La Vénus des aveugles* (1903), in *PRV* I, p. 232.

49. Natalie Clifford Barney, "Lamentations des Sirènes," *Actes*, pp. 239–40.

VI. Paradigm for a New Sexuality

1. Charles Moorman, *A Knyght There Was: The Evolution of the Knight in Literature* (Lexington: University of Kentucky Press, 1967), p. 18.

2. Natalie Clifford Barney, "Double Being," *Actes et entr'actes* (Paris: Sansot, 1910), p. 15.

3. Renée Vivien, "Prince Charming," *The Woman of the Wolf* (1904; rpt. New York: Gay Presses of New York, 1983), p. 27.

4. It is also possible that Vivien was inspired by Gautier's *Mlle de Maupin*, especially the section of the volume in which Maupin is accompanied by a young girl disguised as a page, though Barney expressed a great deal of disdain for this work.

5. Vivien, "Prince," p. 28.

6. Natalie Clifford Barney, "La Belle aux désirs dormants," *Quelques portraits-sonnets de femmes* (Paris: Société d'Editions littéraires, 1900), p. 5. The title is a play on words with a well-known fairy tale, "La Belle au bois dormant" ("Sleeping Beauty").

7. Barney, "La Belle," p. 5.

8. Dianne F. Sadoff, "Mythopoeia, the Moon, and Contemporary Women's Poetry," in *Feminist Criticism: Essays on Theory, Poetry and Prose*, ed. Cheryl L. Brown and Karen Olson (Metuchen, N.J.: Scarecrow, 1978), pp. 143–44.

9. Carolyn G. Heilbrun makes this point with evident surprise in her introduction to *Toward a Recognition of Androgyny* (New York: Knopf, 1973), p. xiii.

10. Mircea Eliade, *Mephistopheles and the Androgyne: Studies in Religious Myth and Symbol* (New York: Sheed and Ward, 1965), p. 99. He may, of course, be using the word *man* as a generic term for "human being," but his choice of words is revealing.

11. Eliade, p. 104.

12. Eliade, p. 99.

13. Natalie Clifford Barney, *Nouvelles pensées de l'amazone* (Paris: Mercure de France, 1939), p. 196.

14. Natalie Clifford Barney, *Pensées d'une amazone* (Paris: Emile-Paul, 1920), p. 14.

15. Friedrich Nietzsche, *Beyond Good and Evil: Prelude to a Philosophy of the Future* (New York: Macmillan, 1923), passim.

16. Renée Vivien, "Sonnet," *Evocations* (1903), in *Poèmes de Renée Vivien*. 2 vols. (Paris, 1923; rpt. New York: Arno, 1975) p. 78; hereinafter cited as *PRV* I or

PRV II. It is possible that this sonnet is addressed to Barney, whose blond hair often identifies her in Vivien's poems.

17. Natalie Clifford Barney, "Salle des pas perdus," MS, fol. 1. All manuscripts are from the Bibliothèque Doucet, Paris. All manuscripts are undated.

18. Natalie Clifford Barney, *Traits et portraits* (1963; rpt. New York: Arno, 1975), p. 169.

19. Natalie Clifford Barney, *The One Who Is Legion, Or A.D.'s After-Life* (London: Partridge, 1930), p. 38.

20. Barney, *The One*, p. 66.

21. Barney, *The One*, p. 47.

22. Renée Vivien, "Epitaphe sur une pierre tombale," *Haillons* (1910), in *PRV* II, p. 256. This is Renée Vivien's last published poem, and it was later engraved on the side of her crypt in Passy.

23. Renée Vivien, *Une Femme m'apparut . . .* (1904; rpt. Paris: Desforges, 1977), p. 37. Capitals in original.

24. Romaine Brooks, *Peter (A Young English Girl)*, (1922–23) in *Romaine Brooks*, ed. Adelyn D. Breeskin (Washington, D.C.: Smithsonian, 1986), p. 76.

25. Romaine Brooks, *Renate Borgatti au piano* (ca. 1920) in *Brooks*, p. 74.

26. Sandra Gilbert, "Costumes of the Mind: Transvestism as Metaphor in Modern Literature," in *Writing and Sexual Difference*, ed. Elizabeth Abel (Chicago: University of Chicago Press, 1983), p. 206.

27. Jeanne Louise Manning, "Rhetoric and Images of Feminism in the Poetry of Renée Vivien," Dss. Yale University, 1981, TS 82.

28. Paule Riversdale, *L'Etre double* (1904), as quoted in Manning, TS 181.

29. Riversdale, TS 181. In *A Woman Appeared to Me*, Vivien attributes everything that is ugly and unjust to the Male Principle and all that is lovely to the Female Principle. Renée Vivien, *Femme*, p. 37.

30. Manning, TS 86.

31. Colette, *The Pure and The Impure* (New York: Farrar Straus, 1967), p. 76.

32. Marie Kuda, "Women Loving, Women Writing," Session A, Discovery '80 Conference, Chicago, 28 June 1980. Ms. Kuda also suggests that the introductions were generally so standardized and irrelevant to the books in question that it appears that the publishers insisted on their inclusion in order to protect themselves from charges of indecency.

33. Vito Russo, *The Celluloid Closet: Homosexuality in the Movies* (New York: Harper & Row, 1981), p. 56.

34. Gayle Rubin, Introd. *A Woman Appeared to Me* by Renée Vivien (Reno, Nev.: Naiad, 1976), p. x.

35. Karla Jay, "Male Homosexuality and Lesbianism in the Works of Proust and Gide," in *The Gay Academic*, ed. Louie Crew (Palm Springs, Cal.: Etc., 1978), pp. 216–43.

36. Colette, *The Pure*, pp. 109–29.

37. Catharine R. Stimpson, "Zero Degree Deviancy: The Lesbian Novel in English," in *Writing and Sexual Difference*, p. 244.

38. Radclyffe Hall, *The Well of Loneliness* (New York: Pocket, 1974), pp. 242–43.

39. Esther Newton, "The Mythic Mannish Lesbian: Radclyffe Hall and the New Woman," *Signs*, 9 (1984), 560.

40. Renée Vivien, "J'ai jeté mes fleurs . . . ," *Sillages* (1908), in *PRV* II, p. 144. Italics in original.

41. Renée Vivien, "Paroles à l'amie," *A l'heure des mains jointes* (1906), in *PRV* II, p. 59. Ellipsis in the original.

42. Hall, p. 152.

43. Natalie Clifford Barney, *Pensées*, p. 4.

44. Natalie Clifford Barney, *Souvenirs indiscrets* (Paris: Flammarion, 1960), p. 23.

45. Barney, "Nos secrètes amours," MS, fol. 230.

46. Natalie Clifford Barney, "Autour d'une victoire," *Actes*, p. 47.

47. Barney, *Quelques portraits*, p. 47.

48. Natalie Clifford Barney, *Eparpillements* (Paris: Sansot, 1910), p. 60.

49. Barney, *Eparpillements*, p. 60.

50. Vivien, *Femme*, p. 106.

51. Vivien, *Femme*, p. 106.

52. Vivien, *Femme*, p. 68.

53. Vivien, *Femme*, p. 41.

54. Barney, "A une fiancée," *Quelques portraits*, p. 47.

55. Barney, *Eparpillements*, p. 6.

56. Natalie Clifford Barney, "L'Amour défendu," in *Traits*, p. 166.

57. Barney, "L'Amour défendu," p. 166.

58. Barney, "L'Amour défendu," p. 175.

59. Barney, "L'Amour défendu," p. 175.

60. Shari Benstock, *Women of the Left Bank, Paris, 1900–1940* (Austin: University of Texas Press, 1986.), pp. 289–90.

61. Barney, *Pensées*, pp. 70–71.

62. Barney, "L'Amour défendu," p. 168.

63. Renée Vivien, "Les Succubes disent. . . ," *La Vénus des aveugles* (1903), in *PRV* I, p. 197.

64. Renée Vivien, "La Mort de Psappha," *Evocations* (1903), in *PRV* I, p. 92. Italics in original.

65. Manning, TS 106.

66. Renée Vivien, "Bona Dea," *The Woman of the Wolf* (1904; rpt. New York: Gay Presses of New York, 1983), p. 121.

67. Renée Vivien, "The Friendship of Women," *Woman*, pp. 101–103.

68. Barney, "L'Amour défendu," p. 176.

69. Natalie Clifford Barney, "Gide et les autres," in *Traits*, p. 161.

70. Barney, *Nouvelles pensées*, p. 200.

71. Barney, *Nouvelles pensées*, p. 200. Ironically, the term *Gomorrhean* has never had the pejorative meaning of its counterpart *Sodomite*.

72. Barney, "Gide," p. 158.

73. Natalie Clifford Barney, "Her Legitimate Lover," MS, fol. 20.

74. Barney, *Eparpillements*, p. 6.

75. Barney, *Eparpillements*, p. 5.

76. Vivien, *Femme*, p. 32.

77. Jean Chalon, *Portrait d'une séductrice* (Paris: Stock, 1976), p. 106.

78. Natalie Clifford Barney, "Le Mystère de Psyché," MS, fol. 20.

79. Barney, "Mystère," fol. 20 and *Nouvelles pensées*, pp. 198–99.

80. Karla Jay, "No Man's Land," in *Lavender Culture*, ed. Karla Jay and Allen Young (New York: Jove, 1978), pp. 48–49. The precise date of the emergence of "gay people" or a "gay lifestyle" is disputed among gay historians. Some, like Jonathan Katz, date the emergence of a "gay lifestyle" in the United States to the end of the nineteenth century. Others, such as John Boswell, contend that "gay people" have always existed.

81. Renée Vivien, "Twilight," *Evocations*, p. 110.

82. Of course, not all models of androgyny are constructed this way, and had

Barney and Vivien known of others than the ones they indicate, such as are found in gynandrous myths from ancient Greece (other than Plato) and Rome, they might have constructed different images of gynandry or perhaps chosen to imitate other mythologies.

VII. Conclusion

1. Elyse Blankley, "Return to Mytilene: Renée Vivien and the City of Women," in *Women Writers and the City: Essays in Feminist Literary Criticism,* ed. Susan Merrill Squier (Knoxville: University of Tennessee Press, 1984), pp. 48–49.

2. Jane Marcus, "Liberty, Sorority, Misogyny," in *The Representation of Women in Fiction,* ed. Carolyn G. Heilbrun and Margaret R. Higonnet (Baltimore: Johns Hopkins University Press, 1983), p. 86.

3. Lillian Faderman, *Surpassing the Love of Men* (New York: Morrow, 1981), p. 363.

4. Natalie Clifford Barney, *Quelques portraits-sonnets de femmes* (Paris: Société d'Editions littéraires, 1900), pp. vii–viii.

5. Barney, *Quelques portraits,* p. viii.

6. Colette, *The Pure and the Impure* (New York: Farrar Straus, 1967), p. 92.

7. Faderman, p. 363.

8. Jill Johnston, *Lesbian Nation: The Feminist Solution* (New York: Simon and Schuster, 1973), pp. 247–66.

9. Susan Husserl-Kapit, "An Interview with Marguerite Duras," *Signs,* 1 (1975), 426.

10. Grahn claims, for instance, that "Sappho's work indicated none of the restrictions, lack of safety, fear of reprisal by husband, police or other patriarchal institution. Her world was not patriarchal." Yet most scholars agree that matriarchies had ceased to exist in Greece by the 7th century B.C., and Grahn herself later concurs with the generally held belief that Sappho was exiled—presumably by male authorities. See Judy Grahn, *The Highest Apple: Sappho and the Lesbian Poetic Tradition* (San Francisco: Spinsters, 1985), p. 10.

11. Annis Pratt, *Archetypal Patterns in Women's Fiction* (Bloomington: Indiana University Press, 1981), p. 121.

12. Monique Wittig and Sande Zeig, *Lesbian Peoples: Material for a Dictionary* (New York: Avon, 1979), p. 43.

13. Andrea Dworkin, *Woman Hating* (New York: Dutton, 1974), pp. 174–75.

14. Quoted in "An Interview with Adrienne Rich," Part II, *Conditions: Two* (Fall 1977), p. 58.

BIBLIOGRAPHY

Primary Sources

Barney, Alice Pike, and Natalie Clifford Barney. "The Color of His Soul." MS. Bibliothèque Doucet, Paris.

Barney, Natalie Clifford. *Quelques portraits-sonnets de femmes.* Paris: Société d'Editions littéraires, 1900.

———. Letters to Alice Pike Barney. Bibliothèque Doucet, Paris.

———, [Tryphé]. *Cinq petits dialogues grecs (antithèses et parallèles).* Paris: Plume, 1902.

———. *Actes et entr'actes.* Paris: Sansot, 1910.

———. *Eparpillements.* Paris: Sansot, 1910.

———. *Pensées d'une amazone.* Paris: Emile-Paul, 1920.

———. *Poems & poèmes: autres alliances.* Paris: Emile-Paul; New York: Doran, 1920.

———. "Les Pensées d'une amazone: réponse à André Germain." *Les Ecrits nouveaux* 9, No. 6 (1922), 78–79.

———. *Aventures de l'esprit.* Paris, 1929; rpt. New York: Arno, 1975.

———. *The One Who Is Legion, Or A.D.'s After-Life.* London: Partridge, 1930.

———. *Nouvelles pensées de l'amazone.* Paris: Mercure de France, 1939.

———. *Souvenirs indiscrets.* Paris: Flammarion, 1960.

———. "Idleness." *Adam: International Review* 29, No. 299 (1962) 49–53.

———. "My Country 'tis of Thee." *Adam: International Review* 29, No. 299 (1962) 67–71.

———. *Traits et portraits.* Paris, 1963; rpt. New York: Arno, 1975.

———. "Les Amants de la poule." MS. Bibliothèque Doucet, Paris.

———. "Amazon's Note-Book." MS. Bibliothèque Doucet, Paris.

———. "Autour d'une victoire." MS. Bibliothèque Doucet, Paris.

———. "Brothers in Arms." MS. Bibliothèque Doucet, Paris.

———. "Faune et phono." MS. Bibliothèque Doucet, Paris.

———. "Les Jours inutilisables." MS. Bibliothèque Doucet, Paris.

———. "Her Legitimate Lover." MS. Bibliothèque Doucet, Paris.

———. "Le Mystère de Psyché." MS. Bibliothèque Doucet, Paris.

———. "Salle des pas perdus." MS. Bibliothèque Doucet, Paris.

———. "Nos secrètes amours." MS. Bibliothèque Doucet, Paris.

[Barney, Natalie Clifford]. *Je me souviens.* Paris: Sansot, 1910.

[Barney, Natalie Clifford]. "The Woman Who Lives with Me." n.p.: privately printed, n.d.

Vivien, Renée. *Brumes de fjords.* Paris: Lemerre, 1902.

———. *The Woman of the Wolf.* 1904; rpt. New York: Gay Presses of New York, 1983.

———. *Une Femme m'apparut . . . .* 1904; rpt. Paris: Desforges, 1977.

———. *Le Christ, Aphrodite et M. Pepin.* Paris: Sansot, 1907.

———. *Poèmes en prose.* Paris: Sansot, 1909.

———. *Anne Boleyn: Reproduction en fac-similé des épreuves uniques de l'édition jamais tirée de Lemerre (1909).* Introd. Jean-Paul Goujon. Muizon: L'Ecart, 1982.

———. *Poèmes de Renée Vivien.* 2 vols. Paris, 1923; rpt. New York: Arno, 1975.
———. Letters to Amédée Moullé, 1894–1895. Bibliothèque Nationale, Paris.
[Vivien, Renée, trans.]. *Sapho.* Paris: Lemerre, 1909.
[Vivien, Renée] Riversdale, Paule. *L'Etre double.* Paris: Lemerre, 1904.

Secondary Sources

Aldington, Richard. "The Poised Lady." *Adam: International Review* 29, No. 299 (1962), 26.
Balzac, Honoré de. *Séraphita.* Vol. X of *La Comédie humaine.* Paris: Pléiade, 1950, pp. 457–589.
Barnard, Mary. *Sappho: A New Translation.* Berkeley: University of California Press, 1958.
Barney, Alice Pike. Letters to Natalie Clifford Barney. Bibliothèque Doucet, Paris.
Baudelaire, Charles. *Les Fleurs du mal.* Paris: Garnier, 1961.
———. *Journaux intimes.* ed. critique. Paris: Corti, 1949.
Benstock, Shari. *Women of the Left Bank, Paris, 1900–1940.* Austin: University of Texas Press, 1986.
Blankley, Elyse, "Return to Mytilene: Renée Vivien and the City of Women." In *Women Writers and the City: Essays in Feminist Literary Criticism.* Ed. Susan Merrill Squier. Knoxville: University of Tennessee Press, 1984, pp. 45–67.
Bowra, Sir [Cecil] Maurice. *Ancient Greek Literature.* London: Oxford University Press, 1959.
———. *Greek Lyric Poetry from Alcman to Simonides.* Oxford: Clarendon Press, 1961.
Bradley, Marian Zimmer. *The Mists of Avalon.* New York: Knopf, 1983.
Breeskin, Adelyn D., ed. *Romaine Brooks.* Washington, D.C.: Smithsonian, 1986.
Brooks, Romaine. *Self-Portrait.* National Collection of Fine Arts, Washington, D.C.
———. *Thief of Souls.* Washington, D.C.: National Collection of Fine Arts, 1971.
Brown, Irving. *Leconte de Lisle: A Study of the Man and His Poetry.* New York: AMS Press, 1966.
Burgues, Simone. Letter to Karla Jay, 24 August 1985.
———. "Renée Vivien et Charles-Brun ou les lettres à Suzanne." *Bulletin du Bibliophile* 2 (1977), 125–38.
Burton, Richard F. "Terminal Essay," *A Plain and Literal Translation of the Arabian Nights Entertainments.* Benares, India: Kamahastra Society, 1885, pp. i–xxxii.
Causse, Michèle. *Berthe ou un demi-siècle auprès de l'amazone.* Paris: Tierce, 1980.
Chalon, Jean. *Portrait d'une séductrice.* Paris: Stock, 1976.
Chalupt, René. "Les Pensées d'une amazone." *Les Ecrits nouveaux* 9, No. 4 (1922), 61–65.
Chapon, François, et al. *Autour de Natalie Clifford Barney.* Paris: Universités de Paris, 1976.
Cirlot, J. E. *A Dictionary of Symbols.* 2nd ed. New York: Philosophical Library, 1978.
Cleyrergue, Berthe. Personal interview. 20 July 1978.
Colette. *The Pure and the Impure.* New York: Farrar Straus, 1967.
———. *La Vagabonde.* Vol. III of *Œuvres complètes de Colette.* Paris: Flammarion, 1973, pp. 217–400.

Curb, Rosemary and Nancy Manahan, eds. *Lesbian Nuns: Breaking Silence.* Tallahassee, Fl.: Naiad, 1985.

Daly, Mary. *Beyond God the Father: Toward a Philosophy of Women's Liberation.* Boston: Beacon, 1973.

Dickson, Lovat. *Radclyffe Hall at the Well of Loneliness: A Sapphic Chronicle.* London: Collins, 1975.

Dreyfus-Barney, Laura. Letters to Natalie Clifford Barney. Bibliothèque Doucet, Paris.

Dworkin, Andrea. *Woman Hating.* New York: Dutton, 1974.

Eliade, Mircea. *Mephistopheles and the Androgyne: Studies in Religious Myth and Symbol.* New York: Sheed and Ward, 1965.

Faderman, Lillian. *Surpassing the Love of Men.* New York: Morrow, 1981.

Ferrante, Joan M. *Woman as Image in Medieval Literature from the Twelfth Century to Dante.* New York: Columbia University Press, 1975.

Ford, Hugh, ed. *The Left Bank Revisited: Selections from the Paris Tribune 1917–1934.* University Park: Pennsylvania State University Press, 1972.

Foster, Jeannette H. *Sex-Variant Women in Literature.* Baltimore: Diana Press, 1975.

Germain, André. *Renée Vivien.* Paris: Crès, 1917.

———. "Chroniques: A propos de l'amazone: lettre à René Chalupt." *Les Ecrits nouveaux* 9, No. 5 (1922), 71–72.

Gilbert, Sandra. "Costumes of the Mind: Transvestism as Metaphor in Modern Literature." In *Writing and Sexual Difference.* Ed. Elizabeth Abel. Chicago: University of Chicago Press, 1983, pp. 193–219.

———, and Susan Gubar. *The Madwoman in the Attic: The Woman Writer and the Nineteenth Century Literary Imagination.* New Haven: Yale University Press, 1979.

Gilman, Charlotte Perkins. *Herland.* New York: Pantheon, 1979.

Goujon, Jean-Paul. "Un Livre inédit de Renée Vivien: *Anne Boleyn.*" *Bulletin du Bibliophile* 11 (1977), 139–47.

———. *Tes blessures sont plus douces que leurs caresses: Vie de Renée Vivien.* Paris: Desforges, 1986.

Gourmont, Remy de. *Lettres à l'amazone.* 18th ed. Paris: Crès, 1922.

———. *Lettres intimes à l'amazone.* 4th ed. Paris: La Centaine, 1927.

Grahn, Judy. *The Highest Apple: Sappho and the Lesbian Poetic Tradition.* San Francisco: Spinsters, 1985.

Graves, Robert. *The Greek Myths.* I. Baltimore: Penguin, 1955.

Gubar, Susan. "Sapphistries." *Signs* 10 (1984), 43–62.

Hall, Radclyffe. *The Well of Loneliness.* New York: Pocket, 1974.

Harris, Bertha. "The More Profound Nationality of Their Lesbianism: Lesbian Society in Paris in the 1920's." In *Amazon Expedition: A Lesbianfeminist Anthology.* Ed. Phyllis Birkby et al. New York: Times Change Press, 1973, pp. 77–88.

Heilbrun, Carolyn G. *Toward a Recognition of Androgyny.* New York: Knopf, 1973.

Husserl-Kapit, Susan. "An Interview with Marguerite Duras." *Signs* 1 (1975), 423–34.

"Interview with Adrienne Rich." Part II. *Conditions: Two.* Fall 1977, pp. 55–60.

James, Edwin Oliver. *The Cult of the Mother Goddess: An Archaeological and Documentary Study.* New York: Praeger, 1959.

Jay, Karla. "The Amazon Was a Pacifist." In *Reweaving the Web of Life: Feminism and Nonviolence.* Ed. Pam McAllister. Philadelphia: New Society, 1982.

————. "Male Homosexuality and Lesbianism in the Works of Proust and Gide." In *The Gay Academic*. Ed. Louie Crew. Palm Springs, Cal.: Etc., 1978, pp. 216–43.

————. "No Man's Land." In *Lavender Culture*. Ed. Karla Jay and Allen Young. New York: Jove, 1978, pp. 48–65.

Johnston, Jill. *Lesbian Nation: The Feminist Solution*. New York: Simon and Schuster, 1973.

Kuda, Marie. "Women Loving, Women Writing." Session A, Discovery '80 Conference, Chicago, 28 June 1980.

Le Dantec, Yves-Gérard. *Renée Vivien: femme damnée, femme sauvée*. Aix-en-Provence: Editions du Feu, 1930.

Lénéru, Marie. *Journal of Marie Lénéru*. New York: Macmillan, 1923.

Lewis, C. S. *The Allegory of Love: A Study in Medieval Tradition*. London: Oxford University Press, 1938.

Lorenz, Paul. *Sapho 1900, Renée Vivien*. Paris: Julliard, 1977.

Los Angeles Record, 13 April 1925, p. 2.

Louÿs, Pierre. *Les Chansons de Bilitis*. Vol. III of *Œuvres complètes*. Geneva: Slatkine, 1973, pp. 1–174.

Mallarmé, Stephane. *Selected Poems*. Berkeley: University of California Press, 1957.

Manning, Jeanne Louise. "Renée Vivien and the Theme of the Androgyne." *Bulletin du Bibliophile* 2 (1977), 151–54.

————. "Rhetoric and Images of Feminism in the Poetry of Renée Vivien." Dss. Yale University, 1981.

Marcus, Jane. "Liberty, Sorority, Misogyny." In *The Representation of Women in Fiction*. Ed. Carolyn G. Heilbrun and Margaret R. Higonnet. Baltimore: Johns Hopkins University Press, 1983, pp. 60–97.

————. "The Niece of a Nun: Virginia Woolf, Caroline Stephen, and the Cloistered Imagination." In *Virginia Woolf: A Feminist Slant*. Ed. Jane Marcus. Lincoln: University of Nebraska Press, 1984, pp. 7–36.

Maurras, Charles. *Le Romantisme féminin*. Paris: Cité des Livres, 1926.

Milly. "Renée Vivien: de l'évolution d'une poésie et d'un mysticisme." *Les Ecrits nouveaux* 2, No. 6 (1918), 17–34.

Monier, Henri. *Dictionnaire de poétique et de rhétorique*. Paris: Presses universitaires de France, 1961.

Moorman, Charles. *A Knyght There Was: The Evolution of the Knight in Literature*. Lexington: University of Kentucky Press, 1967.

Mora, Edith. *Sappho: histoire d'un poète et traduction intégrale de l'œuvre*. Paris: Flammarion, 1966.

Neumann, Erich. *The Great Mother: An Analysis of the Archetype*. Princeton: Princeton University Press, 1974.

Newton, Esther. "The Mythic Mannish Lesbian: Radclyffe Hall and the New Woman." *Signs* 9 (1984), 557–75.

Nietzsche, Friedrich. *Beyond Good and Evil: Prelude to a Philosophy of the Future*. New York: Macmillan, 1923.

O'Brien, Renée. Letter to Karla Jay. 23 April 1986.

————. Personal interview. 6 January 1986.

Olivia [Dorothy Strachey]. *Olivia*. New York: Sloane, 1949.

Orenstein, Gloria. "The Salon of Natalie Clifford Barney: An Interview with Berthe Cleyrergue." *Signs* 4 (1979), 484–96.

Ovid. "The Heroides XV." Vol. I of *Heroides and Amores*. 2nd ed. Cambridge, Mass.: Harvard University Press, 1977, pp. 180–97.

Page, Denis. *Sappho and Alcaeus: An Introduction to the Study of Ancient Lesbian Poetry.* London: Oxford University Press, 1959.

Plato. *The Phaedrus, Lysis and Protagoras.* London: Macmillan, 1925.

Pougy, Liane de. *Idylle saphique.* Paris: Plume, 1901.

———. *Mes cahiers bleus.* Paris: Plon, 1977.

Pratt, Annis. *Archetypal Patterns in Women's Fiction.* Bloomington: Indiana University Press, 1981.

Preminger, Alex, ed. *Princeton Encyclopedia of Poetry and Poetics.* Enlarged ed., 1974.

Robinson, David M. *Sappho and Her Influence.* New York: Cooper Square, 1963.

Rorem, Ned. Personal interview. 29 October 1983.

Rose, H. J. *A Handbook of Greek Mythology Including Its Extension to Rome.* New York: Dutton, 1959.

Rouveyre, André. *Souvenirs de mon commerce.* Paris: Crès, 1921.

———. *Le Reclus et le retors: Gourmont et Gide.* Paris: Crès, 1927.

Rubin, Gayle, introd. *A Woman Appeared to Me.* By Renée Vivien. Reno, Nev.: Naiad, 1976.

———. Slide show and talk on Natalie Barney and Renée Vivien. Oscar Wilde '84 Conference, Toronto, Ont., 1–5 July 1984.

Russ, Joanna. "What Can A Heroine Do? Or Why Women Can't Write." In *Images of Women in Fiction: Feminist Perspectives.* Ed. Susan Koppelman Cornillon. Bowling Green: Bowling Green University Popular Press, 1973, pp. 3–20.

Russo, Vito. *The Celluloid Closet: Homosexuality in the Movies.* New York: Harper & Row, 1981.

Sadoff, Dianne F. "Mythopoeia, the Moon and Contemporary Women's Poetry." In *Feminist Criticism: Essays on Theory, Poetry and Prose.* Ed. Cheryl L. Brown and Karen Olson. Metuchen, N.J.: Scarecrow, 1978, pp. 142–60.

Secrest, Meryle. *Between Me and Life: A Biography of Romaine Brooks.* Garden City, N.Y.: Doubleday, 1974.

Shaktini, Namascar. "Displacing the Phallic Subject: Wittig's Lesbian Writing." *Signs* 8 (1982), 29–44.

Singer, June. *Androgyny: Toward a New Theory of Sexuality.* Garden City, N.Y.: Doubleday, 1976.

Stein, Gertrude. *Paris France.* New York: Liveright, 1970.

———. *Fernhurst, Q.E.D. and Other Early Writings.* New York: Liveright, 1971.

Stimpson, Catharine R. "Zero Degree Deviancy: The Lesbian Novel in English." In *Writing and Sexual Difference.* Ed. Elizabeth A. Abel. Chicago: University of Chicago Press, 1983, pp. 243–59.

Swinburne, Algernon Charles. *The Works of Algernon Charles Swinburne: Poems.* Philadelphia: McKay, n.d.

Tinayre, Marcelle. *Une Soirée chez Renée Vivien (4 Nov. 1908).* Gouy, France: Messidor, 1981.

Venettis, Jean. "Renée Vivien et l'idéal païen (I)." *Revue palladienne,* No. 2 (1948), pp. 44–51.

———. "Renée Vivien et l'idéal païen (II)." *Revue palladienne,* No. 3 (1948), pp. 113–19.

Villiers de l'Isle-Adam. *Axël.* Paris: Courrier du Livre, 1969.

Warner, Marina. *Alone of All Her Sex: The Myth and the Cult of the Virgin Mary.* London: Quartet, 1978.

Weigall, Arthur. *Sappho of Lesbos: Her Life and Times.* New York: Stokes, 1932.

Wickes, George. *Americans in Paris.* Garden City, N.Y.: Doubleday, 1969.

———. *The Amazon of Letters: The Life and Loves of Natalie Barney.* New York: Putnam's, 1976.

———, ed. "A Natalie Barney Garland." *Paris Review* 16 (Spring 1975), 547–50.

Williams, William Carlos. *The Autobiography of William Carlos Williams.* New York: Random, 1951.

Wittig, Monique. *Les Guérillères.* New York: Viking, 1969.

———. *The Lesbian Body.* New York: Morrow, 1975.

——— and Sande Zeig. *Lesbian Peoples: Material for a Dictionary.* New York: Avon, 1979.

INDEX